The BIRTH of the EVERYDAY REAL ESTATE INVESTOR

HOW REAL ESTATE, NOT STOCKS, CREATES WEALTH

GLENN & AMBER SCHWORM

SAVIO
REPVBLIC

A SAVIO REPUBLIC BOOK
An Imprint of Post Hill Press
ISBN: 978-1-63758-415-6
ISBN (eBook): 978-1-63758-416-3

The Birth of the Everyday Real Estate Investor:
How Real Estate, Not Stocks, Creates Wealth
© 2022 by Glenn and Amber Schworm
All Rights Reserved

posthillpress.com
New York • Nashville
Published in the United States of America

We dedicate this book to our four children, Dakota, Peyton, Chasity, and Cruz. To Dakota and Peyton for surviving with us at the beginning in a small two-bedroom condo as we started this journey together. To all four of our children for all the ugly and smelly houses we dragged you through, for the freezing cold houses in the dead of winter in upstate NY, for all the long problem-solving conversations you had to endure, for listening to our dreams and plans when we had nothing but dreams and plans! But most importantly, for giving us the inspiration and motivation to push on, even when we didn't know if this would work. For the privilege of being your parents and showing you that hard work and tenacity *do* pay off. You are the "why" behind all that we do. We hope you learn from our example and pursue your own dreams with the same passion and dedication we have shown you. We love you all.

We also dedicate this book to Nancy Schworm, Glenn's mom. She started working in her family's business as the youngest telephone operator in the world at age eight, raised four strong men while always doing some sort of side hustle for extra income, and is still teaching kids and adults piano lessons at eighty-five years old. Mom taught her sons by her example that nothing is impossible, and she also instilled these two folk adages in them that have stood the test of time:

1. "When a task has once begun, never leave it till it's done, whether great or whether small, do it well or not at all." (Of course, "not at all" was never an actual option growing up!)

2. "He who aims at the sun, though he is sure to miss it, hits higher than he who aims at the ground."

Mom never gives up and is the definition of strength, resilience, and determination. Thank you, Mom, for setting such an amazing example of the entrepreneurial spirit with your hard work, loyalty, dedication, and love. We love you.

TABLE OF CONTENTS

INTRODUCTION

In life, there are macro crises—like COVID, recessions, or the real estate crash back in 2008—and there are micro crises—which is when we have our own, personal crises. Our story started back in 2007 when I had $80,000 in credit card debt. We were in crisis mode; we were both going through divorces, and it was a very traumatic time in our lives. I was in a network marketing business at the time, and if you don't put the work into a network marketing business, your income will drop quickly—and mine was. I was also maintaining multiple homes—the home my ex-wife was living in and the new condo I was living in—and Amber (my now-wife and business partner, also contributing to this book) had her own place that she was paying for as well. There were a lot of expenses going out and very little income coming in, which created this massive crisis in our lives.

Sometimes, a macro crisis can create a micro crisis. When we had the 2008 real estate crisis, it wasn't just a financial crisis in our country, it was a *real estate-induced* financial crisis. Amber and I had two choices: We could fold up and shut down, or we could double down and go to work. We decided to do the latter, because the only way we could make large chunks of money legally was to flip houses. Now, we didn't have any special skills, neither of us went to college, and our families didn't come from money. We were just average people who knew we didn't want to live like this anymore. But we soon realized that when you double down instead of shutting down, it's amazing what can happen; you start focusing on solutions instead of on the crisis at hand.

People look back now and tell us, "You guys were so smart. You really got in at the right time."

And I laugh and say, "We didn't know anything about what time in history it was. All we knew was that we were in crisis."

We didn't realize *the world* was having a crisis. We kept hearing people tell us we shouldn't be in real estate and it was a bad investment, but we chose not to listen to the masses. Why? Because we believe you have to be careful who you take advice from, because you might wind up just like them. A lot of people I talked to weren't wealthy and they weren't overly happy in what they were doing. They were trying to protect us, but they weren't thinking about the bigger picture. They were okay being what and where they were. We, on the other hand, wanted to double down, so we went all-in and bought that first piece of property.

No matter what happens, there are always going to be crises in your life. What is the crisis you're stumbling into now? Are you going through a divorce? Tough financial times? Did you lose your job? Did COVID hit your world? There will always be problems, and you have to make a decision how you want to handle it. Do you want to let that crisis knock you down, or do you want to get back up? Because remember, the only way to fail in life is to quit.

WHY REAL ESTATE?

There are always opportunities in real estate—always. But that idea has transformed from an opportunity for the rich to get richer into a market that not only can anyone get into, but everyone should. Real estate is the new stock market.

For the last few decades, rich, poor, and middle-class people have created some form of wealth by putting their money into the stock market. From trading to hiring a financial planner to putting money into a mutual fund, the premise for getting richer was either to put money into savings, buy CDs, and/or put money in the stock market. But with low interest rates, the stock market was really the only viable option to make any real money. It didn't matter how much money you had, either—this was what you had to do with it to make it really grow.

When it came to real estate, you would buy a home, which became your equity base. You would then pay your mortgage until you didn't have one, and pass the property along to the next generation.

Because of the flipping phenomenon, along with the rise of Airbnbs and short-term rentals, there are now a variety of assets that never existed before. Stocks are vague, but real estate is a physical asset. Previously, the barrier to the industry was money, but there are now entire organizations of banks and investors designed for this specific purpose, meaning there is now an opportunity for regular people to get into real estate and use that opportunity to create wealth.

There's an entire industry available to people that didn't exist in the past. Regular people have access to cash and credit. The loaning industries have also changed. It used to be that you needed 20 percent down for a house and immaculate credit, but now there are ways to get around that. Short-term rentals have changed the game even more because the return on investment is even higher, making people wealthier far faster. People are figuring out ways to have rentals and Airbnb rentals without putting up the capital.

Real estate has moved to the top shelf of where everyone is putting their money. Because there are so many new options with flipping, wholesaling, and short-term rentals, people who aren't doing these things are starting to feel left out. Robert Kiyosaki started to introduce the idea of wealth being tied up with real estate, but the industry has boomed since then, and we need to look at new ways of investing.

This book is a source of knowledge for people who want to create wealth from real estate. Perhaps you want to make money and know this is a major opportunity, but you need some guidance. Or maybe you are good in one category of real estate but want information on the rest of the options. Either way, this book will guide you through everything you need to know.

We're regular people, just like you. But we knew in our hearts that there had to be something more to life than what we had. We were in debt, sick and tired of living paycheck to paycheck with nothing set up for our retirement. We wanted to be our own bosses and have more time to spend with our four kids. We wanted to put them through sports and college, and pay for their weddings. We wanted to create generational wealth for us—and them. Ultimately, we wanted what we all do—both time and financial freedom! When the housing crisis hit in 2008, we were so ready to go for it in real estate that we pushed all-in and flipped our first house.

Little did we know that that decision would change our whole life.

If you know when to buy, how to buy, and how to make it work—whether you're flipping, wholesaling, or buying rentals—and you play your cards right, you can build wealth just like we did. We always loved helping people, so when we proved our model worked (after 400+ flips), we started to do just that, by offering and teaching our successful formula. We wanted to show other people how to change their lives as we changed ours through real estate investing.

Through our Real Estate Investing company, Signature Home Buyers (www.SignatureHomeBuyers. com), we've now flipped over 850 houses and countless rentals, both long and short term. We still actively flip, hold, and wholesale over 100+ deals a year in multiple markets. We have also generated over seventy-five million dollars' worth of real estate business and built VestorPRO, a real estate investing coaching company like no other that also hosts the Home Flipping Workshop (www.HomeFlippingWorkshop. com) multiple times per year, where we've educated, coached, and inspired over 10,000 students to reach their goals as new real estate investors.

This book is the one-stop shop for all your real estate questions. In it, you'll find the necessary tools and tips for understanding the real estate market and how to navigate it, deciding the best vehicle for you, putting a plan together, taking action, and growing wealth in the way the rich have already figured out how to do when it comes to real estate.

The truth is, anyone can get into real estate investing because you can use other people's money to build your wealth. There are thousands of different and creative ways to do financing. You don't have the same opportunities in any other investment in the world.

One of the ways you can do that is through wholesaling. With wholesaling, you make money finding the deal. You put a house under contract to help the seller out of it with a sale and sell that contract to a cash buyer for more money. You're wholesaling to another investor without using your own money or credit. It's one of the things we teach our students and one of the things you'll learn in this book. You can also buy and flip, buy and sell as is, or do rentals, as we mentioned, both long- and short-term. There are a lot of ways to take over people's real estate and make money with it—you just have to know what you're doing—as well as your exit strategy. Where do you want to get to? Do you want to have income every month? Do you just want to make a quick $50,000? What do you want to do? What do you want to make?

There's a difference between wealth and imme-diate cash. You build wealth with rentals. You get immediate cash with flipping. We strongly suggest using both for a winning strategy. We wish we had started accumulating rentals sooner so we would be closer to our goal. There was a guy in the town where Glenn grew up, an immigrant who hardly spoke English, who had fifty single-family units. Back then, we thought he was the bomb! If that guy can do it, so can you.

You need to learn how to look at your invest-ments on a case-by-case basis. It's not the stock market. What you do depends on which method of investing you choose. If it's wholesaling, that's a quick turnover. Flips can be quick turnovers, too.

Rentals—that's going to be more of a long-term hold. If it *is* a long-term hold, are you making money every month, or are you waiting for appreciation? If you're in a fast-appreciating market, you can play that game when the market starts to rise back up.

Regardless, you need to stay focused on those goals. Since there are a million different ways to do real estate, don't chase all the different rabbits down all the different paths You're not going to be successful that way. But if you stay focused, stick to your goals, and get really educated on that aspect of real estate, that's when success is going to happen.

As we said, we've helped thousands of people navigate this process (which you'll hear about throughout this book). One of those students was Lisa, who was diagnosed with cancer when she started our workshop and came to us going through chemo. She had been a nurse, but the cancer left her so debilitated that she couldn't go back to work and was on disability. She needed to get into real estate investing more than ever, even though people in her life told her she really should rest and not let this new opportunity stress her out. But she told us she was doing this because she was determined to live, even though she couldn't work and was scared to make the leap into an unknown world, especially in her condition.

She had no idea what to do or where to start, so we took her under our wing. We guided her, coached her, and helped her locate her first property. We helped her evaluate it on what she could offer, and also helped her to negotiate. We taught her how to find the right lender and get her relationships started with private money. We worked with her on the design of the house, how to position it best, and how to best manage it all. Through it all, she made $58,000 on that deal and gained a new lease on life. We helped her uncover strengths she didn't know she had—confidence and self-esteem, a shrewd eye for finding deals, and great interpersonal skills working with contractors to get what she wants. She's now better, doing real estate full-time, and loving how it's changed her life for the better.

Another one of our students was Jeff. He got started because he was a manager at a credit union and watched many people get laid off. He was stressed about his future and wasn't feeling secure— he thought he would be the next to be let go. When he was a kid, his father got laid off, and that crisis caused huge stress for their family. Jeff didn't want that to happen to him. He bought a couple of houses, and the first one he lost money on, so he kept it as a rental to pay it off in twenty years—not exactly the goal he set out to accomplish. That's when we met. With our help, he learned how to run a flip, and it was completely eye-opening to him.

Another ah-ha moment was when he was going to do a full renovation on a house, but ended up selling for a profit without doing anything. It was a whole new way of learning, making $30,000 without touching the place. He has since bought and flipped many houses and even found a way to make money quickly on run-down homes. He has changed his life to have security. Since then he has been promoted to vice president of the credit union, but he has no interest in moving up in his company. He just wants to work a few more years to get his pension, and then only do real estate investing by his early fifties. Even though his job keeps him busy, he's amassed serious additional income through flipping. (Most people start alongside a current job to create options for themselves.) In five years, he's made a $300,000 profit from flips. His income is around $240,000 gross rent per year, all while the properties appreciate as the rent pays off those mortgages.

There is so much opportunity out there, which is why we want to help you get a piece of it.

Stop investing in the stock market. The real money is now in real estate.

CHAPTER 1

REAL ESTATE IS THE NEW STOCK MARKET

I was born in upstate New York in a small country town called Duanesburg. I was the youngest of four boys, and my mom and dad raised us in a very small three-bedroom home, probably about a thousand square feet. We never had any money to speak of, despite my parents working hard. I didn't come from a class of people who knew anything about investing, whether it be real estate or stocks; it was really just hand to mouth. We used to go to the grocery store every two weeks—only on payday—and my mom used to buy fifteen half-gallons of milk because there were four boys in the family. She had to freeze it so we could use that milk throughout the next two weeks, and we had to use it sparingly. To this day I still shake milk containers, because I think the milk is going to separate just like it did when I grew up.

Mom and Dad always had side businesses and hustles to keep us above water financially, but we never had any spare money. My parents used to say things like, "Do you think we own the power company?" and make us turn the lights off. Or they would say, "Listen, we don't have any money, stop eating that much," or whatever it was. We always knew that money was scarce in our family. And despite coming from a long line of business owners, they were very small, very unsuccessful, and poorly run businesses. My parents were strong salt-of-the-earth- type people who were well known in their community, but that wasn't because they had a lot of money.

Then something happened that changed things for me. Sometime in the '80s, we took a family motorcycle trip from upstate New York all the way out to Pikes Peak in Colorado to visit my oldest brother, who had recently been discharged from the air force and was now building a family in the Denver area. We went out to see him, but also to take my parents' mortgage to the top of Pikes Peak and burn it, because they had finally paid it off that year. Ironically, it was so high up that we couldn't actually see the flames because there was little oxygen.

This symbolic act made me start to ask a lot of questions at fourteen years old. I remember saying, "Mom, what were your payments on that house?" They were $59 a month. My parents had paid $12,500 for that house some twenty years earlier, and then they paid $59 a month until, over time, they eventually paid it off. This made me start to really think about the value of a piece of real estate and the value of my parents making small, monthly payments until they paid off their debt. They got to the end of their retirement cycle in life—and though they really had no investment money to speak of, only a small pension that my dad had from being a butcher for the federal government—I realized the biggest asset they had was their home. They had paid around $12,500, made small monthly payments for twenty-plus years, and wound up with an asset that was worth $100,000.

Fast-forward about a year or two later, and my friends and I were talking about a gentleman in a nearby town who I knew to be a very hardworking person, but wasn't someone I thought of as a savvy investor. He was an immigrant from Italy who was actually playing a live game of Monopoly: he had fifty single-family rental houses, restaurants, and hotels in Rotterdam, New York. I thought to myself,

"That *is somebody who is wealthy!*" Fifty houses was something I wanted to have, too, so I asked myself, "How can I do that?" If I wanted to be a millionaire, I had to figure out how to do what my parents had done—times ten. If I had ten houses that were worth $100,000 each, that would make me a millionaire.

And so began the journey of learning all about real estate investing.

I knew I couldn't afford to make ten mortgage payments every month, but I knew that somehow the gentleman who had fifty houses had found a way to do it: by having tenants pay them off. So I thought to myself, "*Let's have other people pay my mortgage for me.*" In other words, I could have *other* people build my investment for me. That was unlike anything else I'd ever seen in the stock market, and it remains the reason why real estate is so different. In the stock market, you have to put your own money in, be savvy, move it around, look for trends, and watch it grow. You have to make sure that you're investing low and that you're in stable investments. If the market starts to tank or turn, you have to be savvy enough or have enough wherewithal to move that money quickly to another investment. Or you'll need to make sure you have good financial planners around you—but they'll take a cut of the commission to move that money around for you so that you don't lose your nest egg.

With real estate investing, it was the first time I saw a way that average people like my family could actually build wealth. Now, it was only a $100,000 house, but as we sit here today, that house is worth closer to $200,000. And so that theory that I had as a teenager still holds true: The more pieces of real estate that you can buy with other people's money, the wealthier you will be. That simply doesn't happen in the stock market. You don't use other people's money to invest in the stock market, but you can use other people's money to invest in real estate. How do I know? Because that's exactly what people do in almost every other circumstance. Anytime anybody has ever made a large purchase, whether it be a boat, house, car, vacation, or anything that you borrow money for, you are already using other people's money to make that happen. Say you take a loan out for a car; you're using the bank's money, then you're paying the bank back. Well, the same thing can hold true for a house, but you don't need to borrow 100 percent from a traditional bank. (Don't worry, I'll talk more about that in the chapters that follow.)

The stock market used to be the place you put your money to get richer. But today, real estate has replaced the stock market as the place for everyone to invest their money and create wealth for themselves. Real estate used to be something you'd put 20 percent down on, pay it off, and pass to the next generation. But with new investment opportunities like flipping, wholesaling, and short-term rentals—and the varied capital to help you create a profit—there's a new and huge opportunity to create wealth in real estate. It's essentially the new stock market. Early adopters are the ones that make a profit in everything because they are ahead of the trend, so don't make the mistake of letting the real estate trend and opportunity pass you by.

Even when it comes to traditional jobs, I call pension plans a golden handcuff policy: The employer keeps just enough money in your pension to make sure that you have to keep working there. It's just enough to get you to stay, but it's not really enough to let you live a great life in retirement. You can work for thirty years, and then live on half of what you couldn't live on in the first place. This is why real estate is such a better option for the average person than a traditional job.

In the past, in order to be in real estate, you had to *be* somebody. You had to have money to invest in properties, and you had to know the right people. But the game changed back in the '80s when books and information about real estate investing started to surface. One of them that I read early on was *Nothing Down for the '90s: How to Buy Real Estate for Little or No Money Down* by a gentleman named Robert G. Allen. He actually wrote many books on being a successful real estate investor. It was a game changer for me when I read it in the early 1990s. Around that same time, infomercials started to become super popular, and one of the first things I bought back in 1989 was an investing package called the "Cash Flow System" from a real estate investor named Dave Del Dotto. I watched his late-night infomercial and bought his $300 package because I was dreaming about becoming wealthy as a young real estate investor. I had just turned twenty years old and wanted to take on the world. I was so excited when the package arrived and I opened up the box, and I remember on top there was a huge piece of paper that said, "Action equals results, but massive action equals massive results."

That inspired me to start my journey, and I went out and started making offers on properties. Because I was only twenty years old, I didn't have any money, so I took the time to make a full offer on a property with what was called "creative financing," or using "other people's money" (which takes on many forms that I'll explain later in the book). I knew from what I had learned from those books was that there was a way to finance with leverage, and most people hadn't heard of it yet, so I started to make my presentations to people. I wrote the whole thing out and structured the deal with the help of a coach that I had hired. I then told the first guy how I wanted to buy his house with nothing down, and he said yes. I was thrilled; I thought this was going to be a piece of cake. But then he called back the next day and said, "Okay, this is some kind of a con. You're crazy. There's no way I'm going to give you my house without you giving me any money down." And I had to walk away from the deal.

However, that didn't stop me from going on to buy two more pieces of property with what's called "assumable mortgages". The Federal Housing Commission (FHA) used to have a program where you could pay $100 or $500 and take over the payments on a federally backed mortgage, on an FHA mortgage, with no credit check. I did that, and consequently, in the years that followed, I actually lost both those houses to foreclosure. Why? Because I had no idea how to manage them. I had no coaching, no mentoring. It was an extremely difficult time in my life, but I continued to read and study the real estate world. After this major humiliating kick in the crotch (to quote Sting), it would be almost fifteen years before I started investing again myself, but I never stopped thinking about it, learning about it, and helping friends learn from my own mistakes.

I really think the culture of real estate investing changed when books like Allen's *Nothing Down for the '90s* and *Multiple Streams of Income: How to Generate a Lifetime of Unlimited Wealth* came out and late-night infomercials from guys like Carleton Sheets became popular. And in today's world, social media has added even more gasoline to the fire. People always knew that real estate investing was a valuable investment, but when social media hit, all of a sudden everybody was providing all of these different techniques and ideas. People started to share their stories, how they did things, what worked, what didn't, and all the different ways others could invest in real estate, too. The more they saw people doing it who looked more like them—not just bankers and top business people—the more people started to realize that this was something the average person could sink their teeth into.

Because of the flipping phenomenon, along with the rise of Airbnbs and short-term rentals, there are now a variety of assets that never existed before. Previously, the barrier to the industry had been money, but there are now entire organizations of banks and investors designed for this specific purpose. There is now an opportunity for regular people to get into real estate—and regular people are using it to create wealth. There's an entire industry available to people that didn't exist in the past. The loaning industries have changed, and regular people now have access to cash and credit like never before. It used to be that you'd need 20 percent down for a house, but now there are even ways to get around that. Short-term rentals have changed the game even more because the return on investment is even higher, making people wealthier faster. And people are also figuring out ways to have Airbnb rentals without putting up the capital. Now—more than ever—is the time to get into real estate.

FIVE WAYS TO INVEST IN REAL ESTATE TODAY

In today's world, there are a lot of ways you can invest in real estate. When we talk about real estate investing, we're talking about single-family properties, multi-family properties (which are two to four

units), and commercial properties (which are anything over four units). We focus on three to five basic
ways to invest with these types of properties that I
think are best for the average person to get started.
You can wholesale them, flip them, buy them, and
hold them for long or short term rentals. We'll go
into all of these options more in-depth in the next
chapter, but here's a quick introduction.

Flipping (Short- and Long-Term)

Flipping is the thing that everybody sees on TV,
which is one of the reasons why this type of real
estate investing has become so mainstream. Ten
years ago, TV stations like HGTV started to really
show that the average person could do it. They could
go into the nitty-gritty and make it seem fun. In fact,
when Amber and I first got started back in 2007, I
remember watching those shows to learn how people were becoming successful real estate investors.
But we learned they sure don't show you the reality
of flipping! I had to remember that these shows are
for entertainment, not education!

So, what exactly *is* flipping? Flipping is when you
buy a house for below market value (usually from a
motivated seller), improve the property (by painting
it, doing massive renovations, or adding value to it

in any way), and finally sell it for a profit. Years ago, people would flip houses while they lived in them. They would buy a house, live in it for two years, fix it up, then they'd sell it. But, over time, quick or short-term flipping began to take precedence over long-term or lived-in flipping. People began to realize they didn't have to live in a house to make money, and that they could actually do it just as an investment. That really changed the game.

Wholesaling

Wholesaling has been around for over a decade, but it's gotten incredibly popular in the past year or two. Wholesaling is when you put a property under contract, then you sell that contract to another cash investor. Let me give an example: Let's say you buy a house for $50,000, and then before you actually close on that house, you go out and find another buyer that might pay you $60,000 or $70,000 for the same piece of property. You go to the closing table, use the end buyer's money to close, and can make $10,000, $20,000, or more as a wholesale fee just for finding the property! This type of real estate investing has become extremely popular in the hot market of the past few years because there's a lot of money in it for very little work. In fact, we've done some wholesale deals over $75,000 and have students that have made $30,000, $50,000, and even $100,000 without ever actually owning a piece of property—just by simply selling the contract to somebody else. That's what's called "an infinite return," because you don't have to put a dime of your own money in the deal, just some sweat equity.

Rentals (Long- and Short-Term)

Renting has been around for many years. It's when you buy a property and a long-term tenant pays you money to live in it. While it has its own share of challenges and rewards, rentals are a great way to build wealth. What people usually do when long-term renting is buy a house, put a tenant in for a twelve-month lease, and then manage the property or use a property management company. With long-term rentals, people are hoping to make a little bit of money every month. It may not be much after they pay their mortgage and expenses, but they'll make a couple of hundred dollars per month as profit. They also hope to make their money in appreciation as the property becomes worth more. Remember, my parents' house went from $12,500 to $100,000 in twenty years. Additionally, landlords are not only taking advantage of tremendous tax benefits as someone who holds a rental property, but also a lot of depreciation on their tax returns, which can increase their bottom line.

You can also have short-term rentals on platforms like Airbnb and Vrbo. Short-term rentals are something that we took on in the past two years and have been extremely successful with. We actually took thirteen of our properties and converted them into short-term rentals, and all of a sudden, we're making $1,000 to $2,000 a property every single month in positive cash flow after expenses—from something we previously made $100 to $200 on. We have students that are making $2,000 to $3,000 per month on a single rental property.

Virtual Real Estate

Something brand new to the market is buying virtual real estate. We have a twenty-two-year-old son who is very active on the Internet, and he says there's been talk of people buying and securing a lot of real estate in the metaverse. At first, it sounded bizarre, but then my son said something that really impacted me. When I asked him, "How much could it possibly be worth? It's not really a *real* asset?" he said, "Dad, people will pay. It's only worth what someone will pay for it. Just like you say about houses."

I've always told my son—and all my students—that a house is only worth what someone is willing and able to pay for it. I say, "It's valuable because the market says it's valuable." And my son used that same line on me: "Dad, virtual real estate is valuable because other people think it's valuable." As strange as it sounds, even though I'm not invested in it, it's certainly something to look at, because if other people think that virtual real estate is valuable, well, I guess it is to them. I would be careful with that investment, however, because it's an extremely volatile and an extremely risky one. If you choose this route, do it with money you can afford to lose.

Private Lending

Anybody can be an investor. As a private lender, you can loan money in order to make money. This avenue of real estate investing is much more accessible to the average person than it used to be. There are a lot of ways to invest as a private lender: you can pool your money with other people, invest with your time and a little bit of your money, or invest with none of your own money. This will be covered more deeply later in the book, but to give you a general idea, private lenders are people—not organizations—who will lend you money for your flips or rentals with the expectation of making a profitable return on their investment. Some are savvy investors who lend money professionally, but what we have found is that many people did not know they could even *be* private lenders or didn't even know they had the funds to do it! How can that be?

There are many ways to obtain the funds to be a private lender. For instance, you can use cash by using your home equity or you can borrow against your retirement account to get the funds. You can also borrow against a life insurance policy if you have the right kind. If you have an IRA, you can turn that into a SDIRA (Self Directed IRA) so you can invest it pretty much wherever you choose, provided you stay within the guidelines of the IRS. You will use a third party fiduciary company to set this up and keep you compliant. Private lenders can earn anywhere from a few percent up to 16 percent—or even more, which is why it is so attractive. But it does carry risk. If the person you lend to does not pay, you will need to foreclose on the house to recoup your investment. The good news is, your investment, provided you set it up correctly, protects you with a mortgage and insurance. You also do not need a special license, and there is no minimum or maximum.

WHY REAL ESTATE IS A BETTER INVESTMENT THAN THE STOCK MARKET

I really believe real estate is a better investment than the stock market. Why? Because real estate is a hard asset. It's an actual piece of property (except, of course, for that virtual investing we talked about). It's an investment you can see and touch—it physically exists, and it's not going anywhere.

In other words, it's very difficult to lose your entire investment as a real estate investor. Let me give you an example. The property that you decide to buy is insurable, and you always should insure your property. It doesn't cost very much to insure a house, a building that's on a piece of property, or a piece of property itself. Insuring your investment against catastrophic loss is simply something you can't do with a regular stock investment.

If there's a fire, flood, hurricane, or any kind of catastrophic event at your property, it can be covered, meaning you can protect yourself from losses. I have students with rental properties that have burned to the ground (no one was injured, thank God), and because they had insurance, they actually put a lot more money into their pockets. They then decided to sell the piece of land and made even *more* money. Remember: Your property's worth even more money with insurance than without. Once again, since real estate is a hard asset that can be insured, it's almost impossible to lose your full investment as a real estate investor.

Let's say you bought a house for $100,000 and decided not to have insurance (which would be the biggest bonehead move of your life), and that house burned to the ground. Well, the house was worth $100,000, but the actual land is also worth money. So even if the house burns down, the foundation is still left, and typically all the utilities are, too—the electric service, water service, sewer or septic service are all still typically in place. The lot is still a building lot, so that still has value, too. The point is this: You can never get rid of the property. In fact, you'd have to really go out of your way to lose any actual property. You'd have to excavate it and get rid of it. And even *then*, it's still a piece of property. This means you really have to go out of your way to lose your full investment as a real estate investor.

Lending

Accredited Investors

Because real estate is a hard asset, people will lend to you. That's something that they don't do for stocks, or things that aren't hard assets. These lending opportunities are often taken advantage of by accredited investors. An accredited investor is someone whose gross income exceeds $200,000 in the past two years, or has a joint income with their spouse of $300,000 for the past two years. They expect to make that in the next year, and they have a net worth or joint net worth that is over $1 million (that has to exclude the person's primary residence). They understand there's some risk, and are usually very hands off. They invest their money, but also use their time, wherewithal, smarts, and connections to build massive wealth through real estate investing.

Banks

Today, for your primary residence, a bank will loan you up to 100 percent if you qualify for certain government programs. For example, in an FHA program, they'll loan 97 percent most of the time. However, for what's called a "conventional mortgage" with a bank, they will typically want more money down. You have to put 10 percent, 20 percent, or more down on the property, and then they will loan the difference.

Now it's a different animal when it's not your own private residence. This time when you go to the bank, you're going to have to put at least 20 percent down to buy an investment property. However, there are a lot more ways to get it done. For example, hard money lenders will typically loan you more money by taking the ARV (After Repair Value), and loaning you a large percentage of that. This means you don't have to put a lot of money down out of your own pocket. You can also use other people's money, or other people's credit, to fulfill the requirement for how much you have to put down. All you have to know is how to structure the deal for leverage so you can actually get into real estate investing with minimal or no money out of your own pocket.

Personally, Amber and I use private lenders to lend us money to do our deals. We've borrowed the purchase price and the renovation costs upfront on our properties since 2007, and have built an incredible reputation of being solid, strong borrowers. We always pay our private investors back. In fact, they make as much as 10 percent annual APR on their investment with us. We're a solid, secure investment because we're backed by a piece of property.

That's not something you can do in the stock market. You can't leverage to buy stocks. I would never call these private investors and say, "Hey, I got a hot stock tip. Can you lend me a hundred grand?" That's just not going to happen. If I say, "Hey, listen, I think Bitcoin's going to go up," or "I think Ethereum's going to go through the roof, will you loan me $50,000?" they'd laugh me out of the room. But when I ask people if they can lend me money for a house, they'll have a mortgage on that house. Therefore, if I default, they'll be protected and can take that house back. Now that's a different investment; it's secured by that hard asset we talked about. Because of that simple fact, we can leverage other people's money to build wealth with real estate in a way you just can't do with stocks or any other kind of investment. It's really the only investment that most people will feel very secure about once they understand they are protected, they have a mortgage, they have a note, and they have full insurance coverage, too.

Be Ethical

When Amber and I first started back in 2008, it was right after the last real estate investment crisis. If you remember that time in our country, it wasn't just a financial crisis we had in 2008, it was a *real estate-induced* financial crisis. So, when *we* set out, it was the worst time in history to start a business. But we were desperate, had to make money, and really wanted to get ahead.

As we started our business, we would hear all kinds of stories of people that were scamming the bank, so we stayed away from them. Amber and I looked at ourselves and told ourselves early in our career: "Let's teach everybody that you can do this business with honesty, integrity, and character, and still be profitable," and that's exactly what we've done. We've taught people how to do this in such a way that they don't have to scam the system to win. They can play by the rules and still make a great living.

Let's fast-forward to where we are right now. In today's world, bankers are much more accepting of flippers. One reason why is because we taught people how to do it the right way: Don't cut corners, don't try to cut out inspectors, make sure you have everything insured, and make sure you're honest in all your dealings. We also made sure that any people we dealt did it the right way. Every time we spoke to interested parties, we made sure they knew that's the way we did business. Today we're so proud that all the thousands of people that we've taught over the years are still doing it the right way. It's helped to really change the perception of the industry.

MEET DEB

We'd like to tell you a story of one of our students to give you a better picture of the kind of work we do. Deb was a chiropractor who came to one of our Home Flipping Workshops several years ago. She is an amazing person. She is also deaf. She has two hearing aids and reads lips, and doing business was challenging for her. She liked staying in her little world as a chiropractor because she was really good at it, but her hands, back, and feet were getting sore. It was becoming very difficult to do the physical work and stay happy with her quality of life, so she decided to come to our workshop in search of something else.

Eventually, we were able to help her flip three houses and make a total profit of a little over $150,000. Why did she need our help? On her own, she was unable to get bank financing because she was self-employed. When you're self-employed, you usually do your best to take as many legal write-offs as you can. This way, you're not showing as much income as a business owner. However, by not showing as much income, banks don't want to lend you money.

As a chiropractor, Deb didn't have a lot of money because she ran a business and was struggling. She was in her fifties, too, and like most self-employed people at that age, she didn't have any money put aside for retirement. But we taught Deb how to get private lenders and make the whole process work so that she could do it with very little money out of her own pocket. She was someone who really had a lot of cards stacked against her, but because she used the systems we taught her, she was able to dramatically change her financial future. Now, by flipping houses, she's building a rental portfolio with consistent income coming in to support her, and she has dramatically increased the amount of money she's able to put away for retirement.

CHAPTER 2

UNDERSTANDING THE DIFFERENT TYPES OF REAL ESTATE INVESTMENTS AND WHAT WILL WORK FOR YOU

As we discussed a bit in Chapter 1, there are a lot of ways to make money in real estate. Amber and I focus on three main ways: wholesaling, flipping, and rentals. But there's nuances in each one of these that I want to go over in this chapter. Additionally, as we go through this, we'll talk about the different skills that are required for each one so that you can decide which is better for you based on your skills, goals, resources, and what you're willing to do to reach your goals. Let's dive in.

WHOLESALING

For years, every time a property would come up that didn't fit in our wheelhouse—maybe it was too far out in the county, or in a high-crime area of town, or an area where houses were simply not selling for high enough prices to make sense for a flip—we would say no to those houses. I remember we had a lead from someone who wanted us to buy their house, but it was in a rural area that we didn't like. We very politely said, "No, thank you. That's not in our buy box," and we didn't buy that house. What I failed to realize was there are plenty of people that like houses in those buy boxes—I never gave it a thought. Today, I'm scared to think of how much money we actually left on the table—probably millions of dollars over the years—in wholesale fees because we were so focused on what we did and the area we wanted to buy in.

Don't make the same mistake we did. When marketing for properties, if you find one that you can make quick money on by selling it to somebody else, consider that as an exit strategy. If you find a house that you plan to renovate, but you find out you can sell to somebody else without touching it and make a profit, you should consider that profit, depending on what it is.

You Don't Need to Use Your Own Money or Credit

Here's one piece of advice you can't forget: To be a successful wholesaler, you've got to be a good deal-maker and salesperson, too. In other words, you can't be afraid of the grind, of going out and finding those off-market properties. There are a lot of ways we find off-market properties that we'll talk about in this book, but you've first got to be willing and able to find them in order to secure them. Deals that are already on the multiple listing service, or MLS (a database that real estate agents use to list properties and look for properties for their clients), are really not great prospects for wholesale deals because they're on the open market and everybody else in your area has already seen it. When you find an off-market deal and you negotiate to buy it cheap enough, *that's* when you can make a lot of money by wholesaling it to another cash buyer.

The best part about wholesaling—and what makes it so attractive to so many people as an entry-level way to get into real estate investing—is it doesn't require any of your own money or credit. Why? Because you never actually use your own money to get the deal locked down. Let's say you find a house that's $100,000 and realize that the price is substantially below the current market value. Therefore, you put the house under contract because the person's what we call a motivated seller: they have a lot of reasons why they want to get out of that house, which means you can buy it for cheaper.

Next, you advertise, find a cash buyer, and sell the house to that cash buyer for more money. So if you paid $100,000, you might be able to sell that house for $120,000 to a cash buyer. They run the numbers in the deal and realize they too can make $50,000 to $75,000 or more when they do a renovation flip (we'll talk more about full renovation flips later on in the chapter). Essentially, you're getting paid for finding the deal for them.

Currently, our company currently does over $1.5 million per year, or about $125 thousand per month, in wholesale fees from finding properties and selling them to other people or cash investors. Like I said, many years ago we stumbled onto it and didn't make it our primary source of business for a long time. We always focused on flipping houses in the traditional sense, like you'd see on HGTV, and that's what we became known for. But because we became more of a marketing company and started finding these great off-market deals, we decided to start selling those deals off to other people, too.

About five years ago, we realized the market was turning as we started to get outbid on houses on a regular basis. People could do renovations cheaper than we could because we had a full company with salaries, benefits, an office, and overhead. We couldn't compete with one-person operations working out of their homes. That's when the lightbulb went off and I thought, *Wait a minute. Even if they overpay—* because in my opinion they were overpaying—*they still have fewer expenses than I do, so it's still a good deal for them. If they're willing to do that, and I'm good at finding properties, why wouldn't I do that and make an extra $5,000, $10 thousand, $15,000, $20,000, or more selling deals to them?* That also still allowed me to cherry-pick the renovations that I wanted to keep.

That's how our company's wholesale business was born. Signature Home Buyers is a real estate investing company, but we also consider ourselves to be a successful marketing company since our core strength is finding deals. Wholesaling is a chunk of that. We have made as much as $78,000 on one wholesale deal. Now we have students who purchase homes for around $50,000, go under contract, and wholesale that house for $80,000 to another cash investor. Then they walk away with a $30,000 profit, without having to use any of their own money or credit to make the deal happen.

Nothing makes us happier than when we see students being successful without having to take any risk in a deal.

The Best Properties for Wholesaling

You can wholesale residential properties like single-family homes, multi-family properties, commercial properties, and even raw land. There are people that wholesale full-size apartment buildings—buildings that cost millions of dollars. They simply find the deal, put it under contract, and sell it to a cash investor.

With the market being as hot as it is right now, and with so many people getting into real estate, as long as you're a good deal finder, you can make a tremendous living as a wholesaler. But I caution you: Always make sure you do it with integrity. Be upfront and tell people what you're doing and who you're working with (whether it's a bank or a network of cash investors), and explain that the nature of your job is to go out and find a cash investor that will pay your fee. If you do this with integrity, honesty, and character, you'll build a very strong business and garner a great reputation. You don't want to be one of those people who do business unethically, or you'll quickly be found out and won't last very long.

What Wholesaling Requires

Sometimes your business can intentionally start as wholesaling. Again, wholesaling is just finding the best deals. If you go out and find the best deals, you can sell them off to other people and then cherry-pick the best renovations for yourself. It requires you to be a good marketer, prioritize due diligence, and be good at building your buyers' list, because you're going to need a good, large list of cash buyers. Another great way to do wholesaling is to find the cash buyer first, see where they're looking, go out and find a prime property in their buy box, and then bring it to them. Either way, the point continues to ring true: A great living can be made without using any of your own money, credit, and without taking any risk.

Is Wholesaling Right for Me?

If you're somebody who has limited resources, financially speaking, and you don't have any connections that can help you, but you're aggressive in sales and you don't mind going to work, then wholesaling is probably the best path for you. Go out there, find a real estate investor—or several—you can work for, then go out and find them deals based on where their buy boxes are. You're going to have to use your sales skills and tenacity. You're also going to have to be clever, someone who can think on their feet, and be willing to put the work in.

Meet Pam

Pam was one of our students who had no knowledge of real estate investing whatsoever. She came to us wanting to get started, so we helped her with her first several deals. Pam's very first deal was a very small wholesale deal, but it was significant because she bought a property owned by the city. She went under contract, and when the contractor came out, he asked if she would sell the house to him. At that time, she was getting estimates before she closed, and the contractor offered her a number that was around $5,000 more than what she was going to pay for it.

Because she was just getting started and had no real estate investing knowledge, the project was a little over her head. She decided to sell the contract for $5,000. It wasn't the amount of money that was so significant, it was the fact she had just made $5,000 by doing what we call "driving for dollars." One Saturday afternoon, she found a rundown, tax-foreclosed property and sought out the owner. She put the property under contract for $25,000 and then sold it to the potential contractor for $30,000. She made $5,000 without using any of her own money or risking anything. And just like that, she was off to the races. Now Pam is one of our most successful students—doing millions of dollars in business—and we're very proud of her.

FLIPPING

The next category I want to talk to you about in regard to real estate investing is flipping. Flipping has been glamorized on HGTV, the DIY Network (now known as Magnolia), A&E, and many different cable stations. They show people buying a house and doing all kinds of renovations, like tearing out walls, and that's great for TV—and for drama. But the truth of the matter is there are a lot of ways you can flip a house if you know what you're doing. You don't always have to do a full renovation.

Selling As Is

You may be able to buy a house, let's say for $200,000, and have full intention of putting $50,000 in it and selling that house for $300,000. That's great, and you can make a profit, but there's a lot of work and risk that goes into that. There's also a lot of time that goes into hiring project managers, contractors, subcontractors, and everything else that comes with flipping a house. But did you know that, depending on the house, you may actually be able to put it back on the market for an instant profit, without renovating it at all?

One way to flip a house is what's called buying and selling "as is." This is when you find a property that is a good deal, and when you buy it, you realize that you bought it cheap enough to where you might be able to clean up one or two things—or nothing—and put it back on the market and see what it sells for. This works in any market, but it works even better in a hot market, when inventory is low, which is called a seller's market. That's because people are actively looking for a house and are willing to overlook a lot of things. In a buyer's market, when the inventory is high, buyers can demand a lot. But in a seller's market, sellers have the upper hand. Buyers don't demand a lot when it's a seller's market.

Back in 2010, when we put a house under contract and closed on it with our private lender funds, within two days, we received a phone call from the next-door neighbor who said they wanted to buy the house from us. They were willing to give us $10,000 over what we had just paid for it. I had never heard of such a thing before, so I wasn't sure what they meant. I thought to myself, *What do you mean you want to give me more money for the house I just bought two days ago that I haven't touched yet?* It turns out they really wanted this house we had bought cheap in an off-market deal as a rental to add to their portfolio. Additionally, because they lived there, they were willing to pay a little bit more; they had a vested interest in that house. I took a day or two to think about it, and ultimately ended up negotiating for $15,000 and settling at around $12,500. Essentially, they paid us a finder's fee for finding a good deal before they did. Once we discovered that some deals could be sold for huge profits without renovating them, the lightbulb went off and we added another way of investing to our tool pouch.

Recently, we purchased a house for $65,000 from a family whose mom had to move into an assisted living home. They had a deal fall through because the financing for the buyer fell apart. They needed a new hot water heater and had to fix a railing on the back deck, but the family didn't want to spend any time or money fixing anything. They wanted to sell it as is, so we called up and learned they were asking $90,000 for the house. But really, they just wanted to get out, so we offered them $50,000, and we finally agreed to $65,000. After we bought it, we went in and put $2,000 or less into the property for a new hot water heater and to fix the items on the porch so that anybody could get a loan on the house. Then we put it back on the market and sold it for $124,000, as is. We made a little over $50,000 and barely even touched the house! This is an amazing real estate investment opportunity that people overlook *all the time*. We've had many such cases. It's all about how you buy the house. We teach our students all the time: We make our money when we buy a house, but we don't actually cash the check until we sell it. It is all about buying right. Here is a good tip: If your first offer doesn't embarrass you, it is too high!

Another time we bought a home in a neighborhood that we know very well. We purchased the house sight unseen—which I don't recommend for beginners—but we had done over fifty houses in this one particular neighborhood at that time and knew it well. The house never sold because nobody could get in it, and no one wanted to take on the risk. It was on an online auction site, so we put $25,000 bids in on it several times over the course of a year (when you're dealing with banks, always put in offers multiple times). We decided it was worth the risk of $25,000—if they ever accepted it. I knew that for $25,000, even if we had to replace everything and the foundation was bad (and it was really bad), we could still make money because the ARV, or After Repair Value, on that house was well over $150,000.

One day we put the offer in, and they finally bit— they accepted our offer of $25,000. It was towards the end of the calendar year, and I'm sure they wanted to get it off their books. Our team got inside right after we bought the home and said, "Well, this is not in great shape, but it's not in horrible shape." So, we put it back on the market and sold it four days later for $65,000, making a little over $38,000 after all fees and commissions were paid. Amber and I never walked in that property once. Our team saw it one time, took pictures, and put it back on the market only after we closed on it. No work was done, no estimates were done, nothing, and we still made that kind of money. This is how you can buy homes and sell them as is without ever touching the house. It's an amazing way to flip that so many people overlook.

Here's what I recommend: When you buy a house, if it's cheap enough, run the comparable sales or "comps" and see if it might sell as is. In a hot market, you can always try it for two weeks, and if you get offers and it sells, great—take the quick money and move on. Remember, as investors, we're in the business of making money as fast as we can; that's what we want to do while minimizing our risk. Many times, you can make more money doing this than you can doing a full flip and taking on *a lot* of risk. Ultimately, buying and selling as is is an awesome way to flip a house that they don't talk about on TV—because it's not sexy. Nobody wants to watch that; people want to see all the drama that goes along with renovations and flipping, which is the next kind of flipping we're going to cover: actual renovations.

Renovating

Flipping in the traditional sense, or renovating, is what most people understand when they hear the word *flipping*. The sequence of events, traditionally, is this: You find the house, fund the house, fix the house, then flip the house (a.k.a. sell it).

When we do a renovation, we first run what we call a "Home Flipping Evaluator." It's a special spreadsheet that we give all of our students so that they can estimate the repairs on the house. Ultimately, they're looking to find the Maximum Allowable Offer, or MAO. This number helps you determine how much you should offer on a home so you're still protected and can still have a 15-20 percent profit on the deal after expenses.

Here's how you do it: take your ARV (what you determine the house will be worth after it's repaired), multiply that by 70 percent, and then subtract what you estimate your repair costs to be. That'll leave you with your MAO. Using this equation will make sure you're always covered in the event something goes bad or is wrong with the house. Remember, if you buy a house *right*, you'll always make money. That's the first lesson you need to learn about flipping, a lesson that's crucial to your success. Even if you're expecting to make $50,000 but you make a mistake—let's say the house has a bad foundation wall, a bad well, or a sewer line that has to be replaced and it costs you $20,000—you'll still make a $30,000 profit. Why? Because you bought the house *right*.

But now that you've bought the house, you've got to raise money to do the renovations. You can raise that capital with private money or via other avenues, but we'll talk about that more in the coming chapters.

Next up? Fixing the house. To do this properly, we suggest you have a detailed scope of work. This is when you go through the house and lay out exactly what needs to be done, what materials you want, and what paint colors you want—even down to the SKU numbers—for your supplier. You'll let the contractor know exactly where you want the kitchen, what the design is, if you want to make an opening in the wall, if you're going to add an extra bathroom, what color tile you want the tile, etc. *Every single detail* you can think of needs to be covered in that scope of work so it can decrease your chance of mistakes. That way, the contractor can give you an accurate price because they see a detailed scope of work and know you're a professional. Once you have a scope of work, you have to get permits, and then the contractor goes to work. From then on, it's pretty simple. You go through and execute the flipping process, and when you're done, you put the house on the market—and that's when you make your money.

Meet Dan

We've done hundreds upon hundreds of deals—close to 1,000 flips in our career—and we've made as much as $221,000 on one flip. In fact, we have students that have made almost that much on their first flip. Dan in upstate New York was a contractor and making good money at it before coming to us, but he realized that he was getting older and his body was giving out a little bit. Instead of working for flippers, Dan wanted to be on the flipping end. With our coaching and system, we helped him find a deal for $200,000 in his local market. He took on a partner to help with the financing, and then he did all the work on the house. That home sold in one of the hottest times in history for over $700,000. After all was said and done, he and his partner split over $230,000 in profit. Had he not had a partner, he would have made that full $230,000 himself. But even still, a $115,000 split isn't too shabby.

Value-Add Flip

The next kind of flip is called a value-add flip. This is when you look at a home and determine that you can do something to increase its value. It might be adding more square footage—such as an extra bedroom or even a second level—converting a sunroom into an actual year-round living space, or finishing off a basement. (Note: It gets more complicated when you have to deal with heavier construction to fix foundation issues or major wood rot.) These are all ways you can do a flip with value add, but the easier flips are cosmetic flips. A cosmetic flip is when you do simple things like paint or replace windows, kitchen cabinets, or tile. When you're doing value adds, you'll see a property and think something like, "You know what? If I added more square footage to this property, I could make more money." It takes being a visionary to be able to look at a house and do that.

When you're flipping in any capacity, it's always important to ask yourself this question: *If I spend a dollar in this area, will I get $1.50 back when I sell?* Remember, you are an investor, so be sure you invest your money wisely, and don't waste it on something that will look pretty or something you simply want. The goals is to make money, and you do that by adding calculated value, not doing things on a whim. You are *always* adding value—just make sure you are getting paid for it.

Is Flipping Right for Me?

What kind of skills do you need for flipping? You have to be a good manager, because eventually, you're not going to be out there doing the painting, tiling, and construction yourself. You'll have to go through all the hurdles of buying a house (which we'll cover in coming chapters) and then manage the closing process with attorneys or title companies, the contractor and all the subcontractors, the sales process at the end, the staging, and then—*finally*—the closing. There are a lot of management skills you'll need to help them point people in the right direction and help them be good problem-solvers.

To build a rental portfolio, it's the same exact thing—you'll want to manage the process and the property management company, because you don't want to become the property manager yourself.

Do you need quick cash, and do you have limited resources? Then consider wholesaling. If you have some resources, feel like you could pool some money together, and need to make large chunks of money within the next six to eight months, then a full flip or an "as is" flip is what you'll want to do.

RENTALS

Last but not least is my favorite: rentals. Why? Because rentals are how we personally build wealth as real estate investors. Flipping is great, but it's a one-time income. You make great money, but you have to do it over and over and over again to *continue* to make money. If you want to build passive residual income, then you want to start flipping and turning them into rentals. That way, when you flip a property, instead of selling it off to somebody else, you turn it into a rental and rent it multiple times.

One of the reasons a lot of people don't do rentals is because they've heard people complain about being landlords. They hear horror stories about having bad tenants who they have to let in in the middle of the night or who leave the property in shambles. While those stories might be true, if you rent the way we do it and follow what we teach, that won't be an issue for you—or, at least, it will be a very minor issue for you.

Before we even start this section, I have to tell you this: You want to have a property manager rent and handle all the headaches of that property. That's something that we do not do—we are not property managers. We hire out our own and pay a percentage; 8 to 10 percent is a standard management fee per month for all the rental income they bring in, and you also pay the equivalent of one month's rent any time they need to go out and get a new tenant for you to fill a unit. This is a one-time fee each time they do it, and most management companies will guarantee four to six months of rent or they will fill it again for no additional charge. This is not true in all cases, so it is important for you to understand all fees and services before hiring a property manager. Let somebody else manage your rental portfolio like you have someone do for your investment portfolio. It's well worth the investment so you can spend your time looking for new deals. Don't be the person who goes out and tries to be a landlord—there's nothing fun or rewarding about it. Hire out the jobs you're not good at or don't want, like being a landlord, and let someone else handle them. If you do, you'll start to see massive success in your business as you build your portfolio.

Remember how I wanted to be like that guy I knew growing up, the man who worked his way up to build an empire? I thought to myself, *If he has fifty houses, that's $50,000 a month in income.* The good news is, you can do the same thing for yourself. The method is very simple; you just have to take time and plan it out. It's a process just like any way or form of building wealth is a process: You have to do one thing at a time. Start by focusing on how many properties you want to get in the course of a year.

Do you want to ultimately have twenty houses that make you $1,000 a month each? Well, it's a process.

The first thing you want to do is go out and find houses in your buy box. These should be in areas that have good rental income, good tenants, and good schools. Ultimately, the most important thing I want is good tenants, people that won't destroy my property. Next, I want to have a property in a location that will appreciate in value. One of the biggest gains about being a real estate investor and creating rentals is that your property appreciates like my parents' home did over time. Additionally, the beauty is that you're making cash flow month after month on your property while you're also paying down your mortgage, *and* your property is increasing in value. Real estate has increased for over a hundred years consistently, and there's no reason to think it would ever stop appreciating.

With rentals, we use a process that has been recently coined the BRRRR Method. This stands for: Buy the house, Rehab the house, Rent the house, and Refinance the house and then pull your cash back out. Then Repeat, doing as many houses as you want to in the course of a year. If you start doing just one house every other month, in the course of a year, that's six houses; in the course of ten years, that's sixty houses. You could structure that so in the course of fifteen years, you'd have sixty houses that are paid off—if you start now. If you rolled all the rent back into that, all of your positive cash flow, and a couple hundred bucks a month you make, you'll have those properties fully paid off inside of about seventeen-and-a-half years.

Are Rentals Right for Me?

If you're someone who doesn't need to have big chunks of cash and you want to build long-term wealth and residual retirement income—based on real estate, not the stock market—then a rental portfolio is where it's at. Remember it can be long- or short-term, depending on what you want to do.

CHAPTER 3

HOW TO FIND THE BEST OFF-MARKET DEALS FOR MAXIMUM PROFIT

Sometimes, in a really hot market, people think they can make money with *any* piece of property. That's simply not true—picking the right property is essential, and there are a lot of components that go into making sure you have the right property for *you*. If you choose a property in a bad location, a property where the math doesn't add up, or people owe too much, you can lose money on the deal or get yourself into trouble. That's not what you want to do as a real estate investor. Picking the right property is not just about the address, it's about a lot of additional factors. If you don't pick the right property based on *all* factors, you won't have a successful investment. After all, we're investors—we want to make money. This chapter will describe how to properly identify the right property for you and the difference in identifying the property against your rental strategy for long-term, short-term, or flips. Here are some key ingredients that you need to have in order to be successful.

WHAT TO LOOK FOR
WHEN SELECTING A PROPERTY

When evaluating a market, it's important to look for your competition and the big players in the space to see if there's more or less opportunity. You want to also look at inventory, house values, and how things are moving. Are there new industries in the area? Is there a reason for expansion, or is it already happening? Is it an increasing or decreasing market? The chamber of commerce or visitors' bureau is a good place to find the answers to these questions.

When we look at an area, we look for the existing competition, the kind of buying that's already happened, who the marketers are, and the value of the houses. Further than that, you want to look at your own risk tolerance. How much are you willing to spend? You can find good deals in almost any market, but the big opportunity comes in running the numbers on the deal to see if it works or if there's an exit strategy. People get hung up on a certain area for an amount of money, but we say the actual cost of the house is irrelevant if it's a dealmaker. You just need to calculate your costs (buying, selling, holding, renovation, etc.), and at the end of the day, ask yourself: Is it a deal or not in your market? You can go to sites like Realtor.com to see if houses are moving and for how much. Make sure there's enough volume in the area and the overall economics makes sense to reach your goals. Also look at the average rents, and don't forget to look at taxes (which directly impact cash flow for rentals, but not as much for flipping).

Knowing how to identify the right property at the right value in the right market is essential. The neighborhood, taxes, local permit laws, and current rental values are all key pieces of information necessary to understanding whether or not a property is right for you. In addition, understanding how much rehab is needed can make or break your investment. Comprehending the hidden costs you may not be aware of can eat at all of your profits. Remember: The identification of the right property is even more important than the sale, as it typically will determine your level of success.

Neighborhoods

The house has to be in the right neighborhood. Ask yourself: Are homes selling in that area? Is the crime rate fairly low? Are properties appreciating? How fast are houses selling? Is it a family-friendly neighborhood? Is it on a busy road? Is the house next to an abandoned house or warehouse? Or a dump or old dump (we learned this one the hard way!)? What it's next to? (Use Google Maps and do an ariel shot to really understand where it is.) These are all things you want to look at, because when someone wants to buy your flip or rent your rental, they're going to look around and see what the neighborhood looks like, too. When you're looking for a piece of property, aesthetically speaking, you want to go in and look at it through the eyes of an end buyer. What does the end buyer or end renter see? How exciting is the neighborhood for someone buying a house? These questions will help determine how much you can sell your house for and how fast you can sell it.

Taxes

When we lived in upstate New York, taxes were extremely high; now, where we live in Florida, taxes are much lower. Taxes become a factor because people usually have to pay them in monthly amounts. Therefore, if a house has high taxes, that's going to deter how many people will actually be able to buy or want to buy that house from you. In other words, if a house has taxes that are too high and they can't afford them, you're going to limit your buying pool.

Local Permit Laws

Let's say you found a small, 1,000-foot bungalow that you wanted to add a second level to. So you bought the house and were all set to pull your permit, and then the local authorities said, "I'm sorry, you can't expand that property, the code doesn't allow it." You'd be in trouble then! Make sure you understand the local permit laws and local building codes *before* making a purchase. Do the laws allow you to do what you want to do with the property? Now, if it's just cosmetic, you shouldn't have a problem, but you should always check to make sure that you're able to do what you want.

What if you bought a home in a neighborhood that you wanted to fix up, but it was in a historic district? Historic projects are very difficult because they don't just have to meet building codes, they have to go through the historical society, and the society usually wants to keep everything the same. Once we bought a home in downtown Albany, but we didn't do our homework beforehand to learn everything we could—or couldn't—do on the property. It was a beautiful big brownstone, but every change we wanted to make had to be run through the historical society. For example, we wanted to put new windows in the house, but the historical society said we couldn't take out the original windows. In fact, we couldn't do any work on the outside of the house without getting their approval first. We still managed to make a profit on that house, but it wasn't as easy as we thought it would be. This is why you need to be aware of everything you're walking into, and make sure you understand everything to know if it's a good property for you or if it's better to pass.

HOW TO FIND PROPERTIES

Now that you know why it's important to pick the right property, let's talk about what kind of properties you actually should be looking for as a real estate investor. First off, there are houses you can buy that are on what's called the "open market." These are properties on the multiple listing service, or the MLS. You can also find these properties on Zillow, Trulia, Craigslist, via online auctions, tax auctions, bank auctions, and more. The trouble with properties on the open market is that everybody is looking in the same place. Therefore, when the market's hot, everybody is pouncing on those properties, making it very difficult to get a good deal. You *can* get them, but you have to be the first one to get it, and typically people overpay to do so.

However, there are ways you can find off-market deals, and that's the real secret to being successful. If you don't find an off-market deal, there's no money for you to make. That's because off-market deals typically sell below retail value because they have a motivated seller. Motivated sellers are people that have to sell their house for some reason. I call these reasons the D's of the future: that is, houses that are involved with a Death, a Disease, a Divorce, a Downsizing, someone that's Disgusted with the home, a property that is a Disaster, Dilapidated, or Decaying. The good thing is, people that have to sell want their cash now, and that's where the real money is.

So how do you find those off-market deals? You can do it with time, money, or both. There are ways you can do it with no money required, but it will take some sweat on your part. Amber and I believe strongly that you can build your business with good, old-school fundamentals. There are a lot of tools and technologies out there that can help you on your way, but all of them require action, and they all come back to some very basic fundamentals. Let's first explore some ways to find properties that don't cost you any money.

Driving for Dollars

Driving for dollars can be as simple as driving a different way home from work, school, church, or wherever you go on a regular basis. Take different routes home, start to look at the different areas, and see if you find any homes that look like they are one of the many Ds. Dilapidated? Decaying? Deserted (or Vacant)? You can tell a house is vacant if it's in the summertime and grass is overgrown, mail is piling up, or newspapers are all over the driveway. During the winter, signs of a vacant house could be that it's covered in snow and not plowed.

If you do find a vacant house, knock on the neighbor's door and say, "Hey, I'm a real estate investor. I'm looking to buy houses and improve them in your neighborhood. I wonder if I could get some information on this house next door. Do you happen to know the situation?" If you do this right, if you are nice, look professional, and just smile, you'd be surprised what neighbors will tell you—they call them "nosy neighbors" for a reason. But they're not just nosy, they *know* things. If you had a vacant house in your neighborhood, you would probably know what was going on with it. If somebody were to ask you, you might share that information. Whether or not the neighbors do share, you can always leave your card on the front door of the vacant property.

We've bought many houses by doing just that over the years. In fact, early in our career, one of the first houses we bought was a home that was overgrown—so overgrown there actually was an odor coming from it. While walking by it one day, we were inspired to leave a handwritten card pinched behind the mailbox flag that said, "We buy houses for cash," and included our contact info. I had no idea how I was going to find the money, but I wanted to find the deal first, so I figured I'd put it out there and tell the owners I was a real estate investor, even though technically I'd only done one deal at that point. A few days later, I walked by again and noticed my card was gone. Lo and behold, two weeks later, we got a phone call, went and sat with the owners, took a look at the house, and ended up buying it through a creative financing deal (don't worry, we'll cover this later).

Ultimately, we were able to flip that house and made around a $70,000 profit on it. Not only that, those sellers wound up becoming private lenders. At the closing table they received a check for around $60,000, and Amber looked at them and asked, "So, what are you going to do with that money?" They said, "We don't know," and Amber responded, "Do you want to be investors for us?" They did actually become our investors, and still are over ten years later. They've become good friends of ours, too. As you can see, a lot of things can happen from driving around and putting cards on mailboxes. Not only did we get that deal and flip it, but we also got a private lender that allowed us to flip another twenty houses with their money over the years.

That one card produced well over a million dollars in profit.

Referrals

Referrals are when you go to people that you know and let them know what you're doing. One of the biggest mistakes I see rookie investors make is they don't tell other people what they're doing because they're scared they will get shamed, laughed at, or told they're crazy, so they don't share the fact that they want to be a real estate investor. Meanwhile, those people might know or hear about houses from motivated sellers, and they won't even know they should tell you—the aspiring real estate investor—about them.

So let people know that you're looking. Say, "I'm in the market for houses to buy if you know anybody," and tell them what you're looking for—and be specific: someone who inherited a house through an estate sale, someone who died and left their house unclaimed, someone going through a divorce who has to get out of their house, someone who has fallen on hard times and has to move. Maybe they're a landlord and they don't *want* to be a landlord. The house could be in a deplorable condition, and the owners really just want to get out of there. There are endless situations that could yield a prospective purchase; you just have to know what to look for—and what to ask for. It also doesn't hurt to offer your referrals a little something as a reward for pointing you in the right direction. For instance, you might tell them, "If I buy the house, I'll pay you a thousand dollars," because wouldn't you be willing to pay somebody a thousand dollars if they were going to give you a house you could make a $30,000 to $70,000 profit on? Of course you would be.

Networking with Other Professionals

Networking is similar to referrals, but with a more targeted audience—an area even experienced investors commonly overlook. When you network, you want to find people who are going to be in front of other people who may have a house to sell, and let them know to keep their eyes open for you. For example, there are people who have businesses that service motivated sellers. They're not there to buy the house, but they may have a junk removal company, a dumpster company, an estate sale company, or they might be an antique dealer, a divorce lawyer, or an estate lawyer. These are all people who are going to be in contact with motivated sellers. Your job is to let them know that you're in the business of buying houses for cash and can make it very easy and simple for them. By doing that, they will know to give you a call. These relationships take a little bit of time to build, but they don't cost anything. Simply opening your mouth and letting people know what you do and that you're willing to pay them for is key.

Another great way to network is to go to code enforcement inside of local municipalities. They may or may not be able to help you—depending on their bylaws—but code enforcers in any community know houses that are vacant and rundown. At the very least, they can point you in the right direction in terms of where these houses are so that you can go and approach the neighbors. When you network with people who are in front of motivated sellers for their own reasons, ask them to remember you, and make sure you stay in touch with them. Send them an email once in a while or shoot them a text once a month, asking, "Hey, have you stumbled onto anything for me this month?"

If you stay in front of them, you have a much greater chance of having success.

Flyers

Another tactic you can use includes putting flyers around town and on bulletin boards in local community shops. These can be simple ones, handwritten or typed, that say, "I buy houses and pay cash. Give me a call." You'd be shocked at how many people will actually respond to these flyers. Why? Because they feel like they're talking to a person instead of a company. Some people want to talk to a big company, but other people want to talk to a local person.

Targeted Direct Mail

Now that we've gone through ways to find off-market deals that won't cost you any money, let's look at a few that will. First up? Targeted direct mail pieces—or postcards. You might be thinking postcards are old-school—and you'd be right; they are. But do you know who a lot of our buyers are? Old-school people. They still get—and pay attention to—their mail, so if we send mail and stand out, people will call us. What we do is send simple postcards that say we're in the market to buy a house, and sometimes we'll actually put a picture of the person's house on it. When somebody gets a postcard with a picture of their house on the front, a lot of times, they call. Sometimes they're not very happy, but it is legal, and it does make people reach out to you.

Buying Leads

You can also buy lists of leads of motivated sellers, a high-equity list, an estate sale, divorce lists, etc. There are actually a lot of different lists that you can purchase from lead companies. You can also use driving for dollars apps if you're absolutely not going to knock on somebody's door. If you're deathly afraid of it, you can click a few buttons instead and send postcards right from your phone. But remember—nothing beats a good old-fashioned knock on the door.

When you get more advanced in your career, we always recommend taking at least 15 percent of your profits and reinvesting that into marketing to find more high-profit, off-market deals. You can never go wrong investing back into your own business, and marketing is the best way you can do it.

CALCULATING HOW MUCH YOU SHOULD PAY FOR A PROPERTY

A Home Inspector is Your Best Friend

Once you find these deals, you're going to want to use a system to estimate what you can pay for them in order to remain profitable. To do this, when you're looking at a house, make sure you have a home inspector with you. You can make friends with a home inspector or pay them to come with you to your initial walk-through. Ensuring you don't miss anything about the house will be the best investment you ever make. Recently we were negotiating to buy a house when we discovered it had what's called a "point well." A point well is more of a pipe in the ground than it is a well that's been dug. Most banks, we learned, will not finance this kind of investment.

So we almost stepped on a land mine, but because our team is so skilled at looking for these types of things, our project manager caught it in time. In the end we decided this wasn't going to be a good deal for us because we'd have to put a new well in so that the end buyer could get a mortgage. This is why it's so important you have a home inspector come with you on these jobs.

Home Flipping Checklist

We provide our students with what's called a home flipping checklist that reminds you about every little thing to look at around a property, from the outside to the inside (we offer this and other forms for free at our Home Flipping Workshops). Once you determine how much you can buy that house for, then you can negotiate. Remember, we make our money when we buy, so the cheaper we can buy—the further below our maximum allowable offer or MAO—the more money will go into our pockets, period. Keep in mind that every market has different margins; some have really tight margins and are extremely competitive, while others aren't as competitive and have higher profit margins.

If you can make anywhere from a 10 to 25 percent profit margin on a house after it's sold, that's a good margin to shoot for.

Let's say you bought a house for $150,000 and put in $50,000 to renovate it. When all is said and done, the house is now worth $275,000. When you sell that house, after all the closing costs, buying costs, fees, commissions, etc., you should net somewhere around $50,000 to $55,000 on that particular deal. That's around a 20 percent profit margin. So just take 20 percent of the sale price, and that's what you should make on a house. If it's 10 percent in a tighter-margin market, that's okay, too. You just have to make sure that you manage those properties a lot more fiercely, because that will ultimately determine your profitability.

Early in our coaching career, we found a couple that needed help in Denver, Colorado. We found out that in the Denver market, the margins were really tight for flips. While we were making 20 percent margins in upstate New York, they could only manage to make about a 10 percent profit. So we decided to help and encouraged them to do value adds. If they could add a second level, another bedroom, a walkout room, or really *any* square footage, they would drastically increase the value of their house. Another exit strategy they had available was if they bought a house cheap enough, they could wholesale it to another cash buyer because the renovator could still make money on it. Ultimately, in their first five deals, they profited over $280,000 with our guidance. How? Because they were able to find off-market deals, do value adds to create more value in a tight market, and wholesale five of those properties for a significant profit.

This could be you if you use all the methods we covered in this chapter. One day very soon, you'll have multiple deals you'll be working on, and you'll be making your money when you buy houses.

CHAPTER 4

FINDING MONEY—
AND HOW
TO SECURE IT

When people get started in real estate investing, their number-one concern is usually that they don't have any money to invest in real estate. People think they have to have money because of the term "investing." They also assume they have to invest their own money. Therefore, if they don't have money, they can't be a real estate investor. Nothing could be further from the truth, because real estate investing involves *leveraged* money. In fact, most people that leverage real estate as an investment use other people's money.

Now, the truth is, *you* already do this, too. Have you ever bought a house, car, boat, an expensive toy like an ATV, or some sporting or musical equipment?

If you've ever used your credit card to buy something that you paid off over time, then you've used other people's money. Yes, you have to pay it back, but you've used other people's money to purchase it in the first place, so you're already in the habit of doing this.

You can do the same thing with real estate investing—with and without great credit.

While this works with real estate investing, it certainly doesn't work with *all* types of investing. If you went and told your family, "Hey guys, I want you to give me $100,000 because I got a hot tip on a new cryptocurrency," they'd never give you the money. Why? Because it's too risky of an investment. However, if I went to those same family members and said, "Okay, I have a piece of property that I can buy for $100,000. It's worth $150,000 as it sits, but I'm going to fix it and sell it for $250,000. Would you loan me the money to buy the house?" If you can promise them it will be a secure investment because they would be secured by a mortgage, and that it would also be fully insured with them listed as an additional insured—meaning if you defaulted or something catastrophic happened to the house, they'd be fully covered for it—people, banks, and other lenders will usually loan you money on properties. That's because it's a hard, tangible asset that's insurable.

There are a lot of different ways you can use other people's money (or OPM) when looking for financing. But before we dive in, remember that every deal that you stumble onto has different possibilities—some of the techniques we'll go over will work with some houses, while others won't. It all depends on if the seller is motivated, when they want to get out, when they need to have their money, etc. One thing to note: Before you do any of these types of financing, make sure you always have your title company do a title search to make sure you know exactly what you're getting yourself into, including what liens and loans are on the property.

OWNER OR SELLER FINANCING

Owner or seller financing is when you buy a house and ask the seller to hold the mortgage. In other words, you'll make payments to the seller for that house. Now, you might be wondering, "Why would they do that?" One reason would be if they're a motivated seller and they have to or want to get out of that house right away. Recently, our student David went to negotiate with a seller. The seller wanted about $10,000 more than the $85,000 David wanted to pay for the house. Using what we taught him, he went back and said, "Okay, I'll give you the $95,000 that you want. But can I give it to you in six months, as soon as I fix and flip this house?" The seller agreed, which means David essentially got a 0 percent loan. Now, the seller could have asked for interest, which would've been fine, but she didn't. It ended up being a good deal for David because he could now flip this house without having to give all the cash up front.

Here's what happened: the seller signed the house over to David, but still had the mortgage on it, so David still had to pay her. David then used credit cards to do the renovation, and eventually sold the house for over $200,000. He ended up making a profit of about $50,000 after paying off the seller at the closing table—all within five months. It was a win-win scenario, and David was able to flip the entire house without using any of his own money.

Owner or seller financing can be done for the short- or long-term, and the title actually transfers to you or to an entity you're investing with (like an LLC). Another example of this could be when a landlord is trying to get rid of rental properties—maybe they'd like to have the rental income every month, but they don't want the headache. They might say, "Listen, I don't want to pay a large lump sum in taxes for selling this house to you. I'd rather take payments every month." Essentially, it's owner financing, where you can make payments to the landlord instead of to a bank. You can also do the same kind of transaction with lease options, where you never actually take on the title to the property. Let's say you can go to a seller and say, "I'm going to pay you $1,000 a month for this house for the next year." You do a twelve-month lease, and then you have the option to buy the house. They know that you're going to renovate and sell it, and when you do, you can exercise your option and pay them their asking price—while keeping the profit for yourself. There's also a sandwich lease option, where you lease it for one amount, and then sell it to another buyer for a higher monthly payment, and you end up making the money in between.

"SUBJECT TO" FINANCING

"Subject to" financing is when you take over a property with all the existing liens on it. The title also goes into your name, which means you're assuming the risk for all existing financing or liens on the property. This works well when you have a seller who has started to fall behind on payments, or there's not a ton of equity in the house and the seller doesn't know what to do. You can help them by taking over the title to the house so their credit won't get damaged. At that point, you are responsible for making the payments on that house. Here's where it gets a little tricky (though still legal and very doable): the mortgage stays in the seller's name—meaning you don't have to credit qualify for the bank—but it's important to remember that now the house is in *your* name.

Let's look at an example of this in action. John makes mortgage payments of $1,500 a month on his house, but has fallen behind on two payments. He needs to get out of this house, actually, because after the next payment, they're going to go into foreclosure and he doesn't want that. John tells you, "If you can just get me out of these payments, that's all I want." So you step in and say, "Okay, here's what I'll do. I'll come in and start making those monthly payments and take you out of the equation." So while you're then responsible for those payments, they're still in John's name, and you're going to be making them on his account.

First, you're going to have to bring that mortgage current, which means you'll have to pay a little bit of money upfront. In this case, it would be $3,000. John would then move out of the house, and you would fix it up and flip it, all while making those monthly payments. What happens to John's credit?

As long as his other payments are in line, you've just dramatically increased his credit score. To make sure that he's protected, all he has to do is log into his bank account and see that you're making those payments every month, and you get to take over that house, flip it, and sell it.

You can do this long-term for rentals, too. I have a family friend who has a mortgage payment of about $1,000 a month. The loan is still in his sister's name, but we took over the payments with nothing down and put tenants in the house. We make over $2,200 a month in rent and pay $1,000 for the mortgage payment. This is just another example of how simply taking over someone else's payments can be a great way to generate cash flow.

Due-on-Sale Clause

Almost every mortgage has a due-on-sale clause saying that if the title changes in this mortgage and the bank didn't authorize it, then the bank has the right to call that note due in full. Now, I've been doing this for fifteen years and have been in the real estate industry for thirty; I've talked to hundreds and hundreds of investors and attorneys and people involved in these transactions. To date, I have *never* found anybody who has ever had the bank call the note due in a subject-to situation—unless you're not making payments. Remember, the bank is in the business of collecting money. They don't care where the money comes from; they just want to make sure they're getting paid. As long as the property is being paid for, you carry your own insurance on the property, and the seller keeps their insurance as well (which you should pay for), the due-on-sale clause won't be triggered. It's a great way to finance a deal without using any of your own money or credit, all while helping people out of tough situations.

LAND CONTRACT

A land contract is when you buy the house with seller financing but never actually take on title to the property until you've paid that agreement or note in full. Then you can take ownership of the house. The pros for this situation are that it's very easy to take control of the property. One of the cons is that the house is not actually in your name until you complete all payments, so you cannot borrow against it or use it as leverage in any other deals. It's not terribly popular, but it is possible. The more ways you know how to get a deal done, the more powerful you are as an investor.

PARTNERING (JOINT VENTURE)

If you don't have a lot of money, but you have skills and a friend who *does* have money, you can partner or create a joint venture with that person to get a deal done. Always make sure your joint venture agreement is signed by both parties. Now, some people might say, "Well, I don't want to do that because it's my mom. Or It's my dad. My brother. My best friend. My sister. My aunt. My uncle. My next-door neighbor. I don't want to ask that uncomfortable question."

I get it; it's sort of like asking for a prenup—it's *very* awkward.

But here's how I would suggest that you word it: "Listen, in the unlikely event that either one of us is killed or incapacitated, it's important that we have a document in place for our families so this doesn't get tied up in probate. If it does, this deal will be a bad deal. It'll go on for six months or a year or two years, and our families will suffer. So I want to have an agreement in place that explains that if one of us dies or is incapacitated in any way, the other party will take over and finish the project, sell it, and then give proceeds to the other person's estate." In that same agreement, you can also list out who's going to do what, including who's bringing the money, who's bringing the house, etc. Make sure you lay out all of the terms in the joint venture agreement.

You can also partner with a seller. Let's say you meet one named Mary. She has a house that needs about $20,000 worth of repairs and she's willing to sell it for $100,000. You take a look at it and realize that once you put that $20,000 in, that house will be worth about $200,000—meaning you can make some good money on it. You tell Mary, "I'm going to partner with you on this house and set up an arrangement so that I'll take possession of the house, but not the title. I'll have you move out and then come in with my own money and fix up this house. You'll get your $100,000 as soon as I sell the house." You create a contract stating that when the house sells, Mary gets $100,000 and you as the investor gets the rest. Now, Mary knows you're investing money to make the house look better and that she's going to get $100,000 within whatever time frame you set—three months, six months, a year. Give yourself plenty of time so that you're always protected in this scenario. Once you get into the house, use credit cards, a private loan, or your own money spending $20,000 to fix it up. Then you put it back on the market and the house sells for $200,000. At the closing table, it's still Mary's house, so she signs the documents. She also gets a check for $100,000, and you get a check from $65,000 to $85,000, because all the expenses will come out of your cut, including the closing costs, commissions, and fees.

Remember: It's really important to have the right legal documents in place to protect yourself, and to make sure that your sellers are of sound mind. Essentially, they should be someone that you can trust, and be able to trust you, as well.

PRIVATE LENDING

Private lending is how Amber and I have built our empire. We raise money from people that are not large lending institutions, but just average folks who have a little bit of extra money to lend. Now, most of them don't even know what a private lender is, so you have to explain it to them. It's getting more prevalent now, but when Amber and I first started raising money, people didn't like real estate—they were scared of it—and they didn't understand that they could make great returns by lending money. One reason for that was because it was 2008 and the market was crashing. It wasn't just a financial crisis in America—it was a real estate crisis, too, making it a terrible time to be a real estate investor.

Back in 2008, we had just finished our first flip and had two more under contract to buy. Back then we were able to get a bank loan for the purchase price, but they wouldn't lend us money for any renovation costs. When the market crashed, however, all real estate lending was put on hold, so at an institutional level, there was no money available for us to flip houses. All of a sudden, we found ourselves with two contracts and deposits for two houses—but no money.

We didn't know what we were going to do.

So I started to ask my family and friends for help. I put together a package that showed who we were, what we'd done (at that point, we had flipped one house), and what we planned to do. I typed up our goals, how we wanted to give back to charities, put a picture of our recent deal, and showed them what was in it for them, and what we could do for them. We said we were willing to return 10 percent to 14 percent of the investor's money depending on the deal, and back it with a mortgage and insurance so they were fully protected.

But here's what set me apart from everybody else: I never straight up asked them for their money, because that's when people tend to resist. How many times do you walk through a mall and somebody reaches out a little perfume pack and says, "Do you want a free sample?" What's the first thing you say? "Nope, no, thank you." They could be passing out bars of gold and we'd back up and say, "No, no, no. I'm all set." When we perceive people as forcing something on us, we don't want anything to do with it; that's just human nature. So, instead of forcing investing on anybody, I sent out (FedEx to class it up) our nice ten-page brochure packet with a letter that said, "I'm sending this because I know you know a great deal when you see one. If you would please share this with anybody that you think might want to be an investor, I would appreciate it. Thank you."

Home Equity

One of our very good friends heard what we were doing and said, "Boy, I wish I had money to invest." This particular friend did a lot of sweat equity, meaning they were always doing work on their house and making it more beautiful. People who do this tend to create value because they're making it worth more money. So, I called her and said, "Do you have home equity?" She responded, "I think so." I then said, "Your house is probably worth at least $400,000. What do you owe on it?" She replied, "We probably owe around $200,000." (They actually owed less.) I then asked if they had a line of credit, and how much their rate was—it was 4 percent. Finally, I asked, "What if you loaned us $100,000 and we paid you 14 percent to borrow that money?" Keep in mind, that wasn't even her money *and* we would be making her mortgage payments of about $300 every month. She said, "Wait a minute. I'm going to make 10 percent on money that's not even mine?" I answered, "How about that?"

And so she became our very first investor. And she used her home equity—somebody else's money—to loan *us* money.

Self-Directed IRA

To finish financing the deal, I received a phone call in response to one of those packets I sent out. A guy I had worked with said, "Hey, what is this you're doing?" I answered, "Well, I'm going to be a real estate investor. Who do you know that can help?" He said, "A lot of people, but what about me?" He and his wife ended up investing $400,000 of their self-directed IRA money into three houses. These investors are still my good friends, still investing to this day—some fourteen years later—and are still making a solid 10 percent return on their money. They love that we are partners in this together.

We've now raised over $5 million in private lender funds. How have we been able to do this? Reputation is everything. From the day you start looking for investors, manage your reputation. That means even if you buy a bad house, you still pay your investors. Even if you're not going to make the profit you project, or you made a lot of mistakes and you're going to lose money, make sure you always pay your investor what you're supposed to pay them. If you do that and do it right, they will come back to you time and time again. This is why private lending is a very powerful way to build your nest egg. It usually doesn't require credit checks or any of your own money, and it allows you to borrow for the purchase price *and* renovation of a property. Once you build up your reputation, all you'll have to do is send a text or email and you'll get the money wired to your account. Of all the ways you can secure financing, always strive for private lending. It's not always the cheapest, but it's the easiest money you'll get. On top of that, you'll help average people build their portfolio while you build your own.

You'll be leveraging their money to build your own wealth.

CREDIT

Not one of the financing options we've discussed so far requires your own credit. Now, if you *have* good credit, you have more options than people that don't, but that doesn't mean you'll necessarily have to use it for any of your deals. In other words, just because you have excellent credit, it doesn't mean you shouldn't use these methods, since they're powerful ways to have access to money. Remember the golden rule? He who has the gold makes the rules? Well, in real estate investing, I believe the golden rule is, "He who has access to the most money wins." So, while you can use credit cards to buy your materials, pay your car contractors, and take cash advances, it's best to combine that with other methods.

HARD MONEY LENDING

Institutional hard money lenders are willing to loan you money, but if you're a new flipper, then you're a higher risk and will therefore pay anywhere from 10 percent to 16 percent annually or more. These institutional lenders are designed to loan money at a higher risk because their investors are willing to take a higher risk. Why? Because they know their money is secured by real estate. Hard money lenders will loan you a large percentage of the purchase price, and sometimes as much as 100 percent of the renovation costs, which makes them a great way to secure money. You're going to have to come up with some money yourself, too, but if you have the right lender, they won't care if you borrow it or whatever method you use to get it.

BANKS

Banks will loan you money, too, but their terms really aren't that great. You can only get a handful of loans in your personal name—about ten max—which means they limit how many houses you can have. A bank will loan you usually 80 percent of purchase price and nothing on renovation, whereas hard lenders will loan you 80 to 90 percent of purchase price and up to 100 percent of the renovation costs. This means hard lenders are more invested with you to see the whole project through, compared to a bank. This is why traditional banks are not the best way to go. They *are* a good option when you're refinancing, however, which we'll talk about later in the book.

INTEREST RATES

Let's talk about interest rates for a minute. If it's 12 percent, people get very nervous because they compare it with regular mortgage rates, which as of this writing, are over 5 percent. If you're thinking to yourself, "I'm going to borrow money at 5 percent," you have to know that it's not the same market—you're comparing apples to oranges. The regular mortgage market is different from the private lending or real estate investing market; it costs more money because your investors are taking more of a risk. What's important to remember is that it's a short-term loan. Therefore, you're comparing a 3 percent, thirty-year mortgage to a 12 percent, six-month mortgage (it's typically a 12 percent APR, or annual percentage rate). So if you only use that money for six months, you're essentially paying 6 percent on that money. The bottom line is, you have to look at the entire deal.

Let's say your credit isn't that great and the best loan you can get is 15 percent. You only pay for the time you use the property or use the money, but maybe your lender has a one year minimum. Therefore, you have to hold a house for a whole year and borrow $100,000 at 15 percent. You might think that's outrageous, but let's look at the whole picture: What if your flip was designed so that even with the $15,000 in money costs, you could walk away with a profit of $50,000? Of course, it would be better if your money cost was $10,000 or $5,000, but if that's the best lender you can find, take it. After all, if you walk away from the deal, somebody else will come up within seconds and snatch it away from you. Remember: You have to think like an investor. You also have to ask yourself: *What is the end game?* The end game is profit, because you're an investor. If you're not using your own money and are paying someone else to risk theirs, let them earn a higher interest rate—especially if you can make a $50,000 profit. That's exactly how investors need to think, and it's the most crucial part about being an investor.

MIX AND MATCH

Money is everywhere—you just have to know where to look for it and how to structure the deal. The good news is that you can combine multiple methods we've discussed in this chapter to structure any deal and get it done. You've got to be resourceful, though, or you won't be a great real estate investor. You've got to be thinking all the time, *What's the best way to get this deal done so the seller's happy and I'm happy?* Next, you have to make sure you have the right paperwork in place to protect yourself. Therefore, no matter what happens—for example, if the deal goes south or there's a natural disaster—you're protected and you know exactly what you're liable for. Not having money should no longer ever be an excuse for you not to start, because you'll never have to use your own money. If you choose to do that down the road, if you do want to invest your own money, you certainly can, but you'll always be limited on growth. That's why I recommend using other people's money to do flips. As you start making money, you can then start reinvesting in other flippers yourself and making 10 percent to 14 percent on your profits.

If you have your own home, you'll be able to pay down your mortgage, as you're building your portfolio and your property is appreciating in value. This creates value at both ends. The balance is going down on the mortgage, while the value of your property is increasing. As this happens, more and more wealth is created in your house. If you're also building a rental portfolio and flipping at the same time, then you're already creating equity along the way. Over the course of a few years, you'll open your eyes one day and realize you've been paying down houses and they've been appreciating in value. Then you'll be able to take loans out against your own properties at 3 percent or 4 percent, whatever the lowest rate is. You'll even be able to use your own money to fund your deals if you choose to.

Remember: whoever has access to money is the one who wins.

CHAPTER 5

UNDERSTANDING WHOLESALING

A decade ago, wholesaling really wasn't that popular, and almost nobody did it. We used to do a little bit here and there, but now we do well over a million dollars a year in wholesale gross profits. Our very first wholesale we ever did, we got a phone call about a house that was in the inner city and in poor condition. My salesman said, "The owner said she wants a dollar for the house. What should we offer her, a thousand dollars?" I said, "No, we should offer her a dollar. She said she wants a dollar." He said, "You can't pay a dollar for a house!" I replied, "The heck we can't. Of course we can pay a dollar for a house! That's what she wants!" Now someone might be wondering, why would somebody want to sell a house for a dollar?

It was because of the property tax she was paying, the maintenance costs she had, and the risks associated with the house. It was costing her thousands to maintain it and she just wanted out! We ended up putting the house under contract for one dollar, and on the line stating who was going to buy the house, I simply put the name of our company and the phrase "and/or assigns." That gave me the legal right to assign that contract to somebody else.

I briefly mentioned before that the number-one mistake that we made early on in our career was turning down leads because they didn't fit into our perfect little buy box. This was one of those houses. It wasn't in an area that we wanted to renovate in, so I almost walked away from the deal. After going under contract for a dollar, I said, "Look, I don't think it's for me, but I think I have some other people that might want to buy this." I actually paid someone a hundred dollars to go in and clean it out. Once they were done, we saw the structure was pretty solid. I put it on the market and a family that lived nearby came to me wanting to buy it. I was asking for $10,000, and they offered me $5,000. I went to their house on Christmas Eve, the family gave us a check for $5,000, and I signed the contract over to them. When we went to closing, we made $4,999 on that deal, because the family paid for all the closing costs. All I did was find a house, put it under contract for a dollar, and sell it to somebody else.

This happened well over ten years ago, when we were just getting started in our business, and I continued to turn my nose up at these types of properties. I still didn't see the value in doing wholesaling on a regular basis. My wife Amber, however, continued to push me, telling me, "We've got to do more of these wholesales." These days, every time I talk to an accountant or a financial advisor, they look at my books and say, "You do all these renovations and I see you make money, but there's a lot of risk and it takes a long time to make that money. But these deals you've done over here, these few wholesales, you're telling me you don't use any of your own money or your own credit? You're making $5,000 and $10,000 apiece, and you've done five or ten of them this year? Why don't you do more of those?" I usually answered, "Because I don't want to feel like I'm a used car salesman. I want to feel like I'm a flipper." I kept telling myself a story that I wasn't providing any value by wholesaling, and I was dead wrong.

In fact, as the years passed, we went from doing $50,000 a year to $100,000 a year thanks to wholesaling.

And we didn't stop there. Back in 2013, we did over $440,000 in one year on wholesaling. That completely changed our bottom line, and I realized that I wasn't a used car salesman—I was finding deals. I could discover off-market deals and sell them to other people who were willing to pay a premium for them, because they didn't have a marketing or sales department like I had. They couldn't go out and do what I was doing, nor did they have the time or the desire. They just wanted to buy houses to renovate, so I decided to get those houses for them. But I couldn't help but wonder: *Why would they want to pay more than I paid for the house?* The bottom line is that when they ran *their* numbers, they could still make a $30,000 to $50,000 profit even after me making $10,000 to $20,000 on the same property.

Finally it started to make sense why I was helping other investors find properties.

Three years ago, I hired a coach who had a big business doing wholesaling—he earned millions every year. When I first asked him to be my coach, he said no, but I was persistent. He actually opened a coaching business, and I paid him over $20,000 to coach me on what he did. I only spent about six weeks with him, but those six weeks completely changed my perception of how wholesaling is supposed to work.

Once I got my hands on the right contract, knew the right way to do it, and had the right team in place, everything changed. We went from doing a few hundred thousand dollars a year to over a million. This year alone we'll probably do over $1.5 million on wholesale spreads. That includes opening up in multiple markets. Wholesaling at this scale allows us to be a very different type of business. Now, any lead that comes in our door, we don't just turn our nose up at it and say, "This is not in our area. This is not in our buy box." Instead, we say, "This is not in our buy box, but I have people that I think will want to buy this from me. So, I'm going to put it under contract then go out and see if I can get someone to buy it from me."

At the end of the day, the seller really doesn't care, because they still get their money.

We've had success, but it wasn't a million-and-a-half dollars a year overnight. It started with one deal in a not-so-great area for $4,999. However, I realized that if I could do it once, I could do it again. But one of the misconceptions people have about wholesaling is that it's easy. They think, "Well, if you're buying and selling and there's no credit and there's no money, then it must be a piece of cake." Sure, in theory, it's simple, but in reality, it's not that easy.

What people don't realize is that you've got to be a great matchmaker and dealmaker. You've also got to be able to navigate the entire thing and see the deal through. You're not just a salesperson; you actually have to keep the deal together and make it work.

First, find the property that you have to sell. When you come across those off-market deals, you have to buy them really, really cheap (I'll cover that more in Chapter 9). When you learn how to negotiate, you can buy those houses fairly inexpensively. Remember: The cheaper you buy it, the more exit strategies you have—including wholesaling. Sometimes, if you pay a little too much for the house, you can renovate it and make a profit of $20,000 to $40,000, but there's not enough meat on the bone for you to wholesale it to somebody else.

Again, it appears easy, but you have to become a master here. I recommend that, as your first item of business after finding the deal, you go find a buyer—especially if you're new to this. Look for people who are cash buyers—they're not hard to find. Check the county records and see who's paying cash for houses, or go online and check out your local investment groups. You want to find a few cash buyers in your area and ask them what their buy box is. Are they out there wholesaling properties themselves?

Do they just want to renovate? There are also people that are what's called "turnkey investors." These people buy houses, fix them up, and sell them to landlords. In short, people buy from wholesalers all the time, nationwide. There are also always institutions that are buying, so there are some large players in the industry leveraging institutional money.

Once you've found the deal, bought it cheap enough that you're comfortable in your negotiations, and sold it to a cash buyer, you have to have the right paperwork in place to protect the deal, because you don't want someone to cut you out of it and go directly to the seller themselves—which some dishonest investors will do. But those ones never last. Once you get through that, you have to get to closing. Sometimes these houses are challenging because the seller has their own challenges. Now, if you're a motivated seller and you've gotten yourself into a bad situation financially, typically you've made a lot of other bad decisions in other areas of your life. Not always, but sometimes that's the case. If it is, they may have other issues, as well, so you will have to help those people navigate to the finish line. You may become a therapist at times, because people get upset and you have to navigate that. But make sure the buyers are happy, the sellers are happy, and that you get to the closing table.

Every now and again, you may get lucky and have an end user buy the house who wants to live there, and they're willing to pay more cash to you to make it happen. Let's say you go out and do some door knocking. You don't do any fancy marketing or TV advertising; instead you use some very basic tactics to find a house that's off-market. Using our Home Flipping Evaluator, you find out that in order for it to be a successful flip for you, you'll have to pay $75,000 for the house to flip it and make a 15 percent to 20 percent profit. Now, if you want to wholesale that same property, you'd have to buy it below that number. If you could pay $75,000 and make a profit, so could somebody else, so you want to try and buy that house for $50,000 or $45,000. In other words, you have to buy it cheap enough so there's enough money in it for someone else to flip.

Let's say you find a house and go under contract for $50,000. Next, you want to gain access to the property and have your buyer look at the house. I encourage you to let people know that you're going to be letting your other investors walk through the property with you. Tell them, "Listen, I need to walk through with my other investors. Can I please have access to the house? Can I have a key? Can I put a lockbox on?" I recommend that you not be dishonest about this. I don't like when other wholesalers are dishonest. Many years ago, when we first got started, somebody took me through a house that they were wholesaling. Then they turned to me and said, "If anybody asks, just tell them that you're my contractor." I looked at him and replied, "I am not going to lie while I'm here. Just don't put me in a situation where they're going to ask. Keep me away from the seller, and everything will be fine."

Now, remember that your contract has a closing date. Let's say you set your closing date for one month out. Well, you better go to work on day one and start calling all your buyers and walking them through that house. I would recommend that you put together a prospectus to show them the details of the house. What's the square footage? What's the size? You better have a lot of pictures and a video, too, if you can. You want to market the house really well so your buyers know, walking in the door, that this could be a good deal for them. Even do a prospectus to show them what they could make. If you estimated you were going to pay $75,000 for it, then maybe you ask $85,000 for it and see if they want to pay a little more. You're under contract for $50,000 and you're asking $85,000, knowing they might negotiate you back to $75,000 or $70,000.

Whatever the number might be, you want to get more than you went under contract for.

Once you have access to the house, you can schedule showings and take people through the property. If you can schedule multiple showings at the same time so they know that there are more people than just them looking at the house, that will help you increase the price. Next, you have to have the right paperwork in place to have them sign a contract. The contract would be for your price on the house. Now, our contracts list out *our* price—that's inclusive of our fee and the actual buy price that we're supposed to pay at closing—therefore, the buyer doesn't know what our fee is until the closing table. We don't discuss the fee upfront. We simply focus on the value of the house. The buyer then signs the contract, and it's *their* money they bring to the table—not yours. You don't even have to have any money on a contract. You just have to check with your state—you may have to put a hundred dollars down or something as a deposit, but you may not have to.

In our state, we don't actually put any money down with the seller. We just have a contract.

After the contract is signed, we send it off to our title company or attorney. Attorney states are very difficult, however. In fact, they're *much* more difficult than title states. That's because sometimes attorneys like battling and going back and forth, making things a lot more complicated than they actually are. Whatever happens, make sure you keep everybody happy until they get to the closing table. Once there, you probably won't even have to be there; you can either have your attorney or the title company represent you. They will usually have the sellers sign the paper in the morning and the buyers sign the papers an hour later, to keep them apart. Then the buyer wires the money. If they are in the same office, they'll be in different rooms, and the attorney will go back and forth. In this scenario, if you put the house under contract for $50,000 and you then find a buyer for $75,000, you don't bring any money to the table because the buyer is the one that brings their $75,000 in cash. They then wire that to the closing attorney or title company at the closing table.

Remember the split: $50,000 goes to the seller, because that's what they agreed to sell the house for, and the remaining $25,000 is yours. The actual house goes to the buyer. I may be oversimplifying the process here a bit, but that really is what happens on a regular basis. Again, there are a lot of personalities and challenges to navigate in each situation. It sounds easier than it is, but your return on investment from wholesaling is infinite. Because you don't put any of your own money in, you're truly finding other people's property and then selling it. It's what we call "linear income"—income that requires repeated action over and over again to keep it coming in—but you can still make great money from it.

The guy that sold us our office building in upstate New York was a wholesaler. We spent over $400,000 renovating our office, and when he came to the open house to celebrate, he came up to me and said, "Glenn, do you remember the property in Rotterdam that was kind of rundown?" "Yeah," I said. "My lawyer gave me a tip on it. He said that CVS was looking to buy that lot." It was about the size of a block, so he went and put it under contract with the seller for $50,000. He then contacted CVS, and CVS bought that plot of land from him for $250,000. He made $200,000 on a wholesale deal on land that he never owned, all because he had his attorney as a referral to help him find off-market deals. I have personally never done a deal for $200,000, but that is a great goal to have. He also found a commercial deal and sold it off to them, and there's a lot of money you can make that way too. You can even sell to large hedge fund institutions that are buying single- family homes like crazy right now.

To summarize: You want to find a property that's way off-market, that's way undervalued, and then look for those amazing cash investors. Look for people who are paying for properties in your area and don't be afraid to look for institutional buyers that you see online, as well. Many people make a great living selling to these large hedge funds that are buying houses all over the country, and that's certainly something else that you can do, too.

DOS AND DON'TS

Do be diligent with your marketing; follow-up is everything. Once you get or find a hot lead, you have to follow up and follow up and follow up. Recently, our student Alicia found a great lead and we were trying to help her lock the deal down. I was guiding her to do a wholesale and make $20,000 or $30,000. She could have made $40,000 or $50,000 as a flip, but as investors, we're in the business of making money as fast as we can. If we could make $20,000 or $30,000 for doing some paperwork and sales as opposed to making $50,000. for six months' worth of renovations, I would take the $20,000 or $30,000 all day. The seller wanted $90,000, but I was trying to encourage Alicia to buy it for a lot cheaper, so she called and made an offer of $70,000.

Afterwards, I kept asking her, "Have you followed up?" She said, "Well, I followed up twice, but I don't want to bother her anymore." "Text her right now," I said. "Yeah, but I don't want to bother her." "Text her right now." She texted her again and said, "Hey, I just wanted to follow up. I hadn't heard from you for a week or so." She said the woman finally responded back and said, "You know, it's just about the numbers. I just didn't like your offer at $70,000." Now, they're at least negotiating. If she hadn't followed up, that seller would have eventually called somebody else. This is why you have to do it. People don't love selling their houses for cheaper than they think they're worth, naturally. So sometimes, they just have to be reminded of their pain to sell. When they finally feel enough of that pain, they'll finally sell the house. When they do, you want to make sure that they know who to call—*you*. You've got to make sure that you're there. That's a crucial error so many people make in real estate investing—they don't follow up.

Do consider your options. If you buy a house cheap enough, you now have multiple options. You could wholesale it, you could flip it and make even more money, or you could turn it into a rental—long-term or short-term. Get good at this wholesaling piece, and it can be the foundation for your business by providing lots of cash flow. Follow up, stay the course, be a good listener, don't lose your cool, and help people by becoming a problem solver: "Mr. and Mrs. Seller, how can I help you get out of this situation today? How can I help you through this?" "Mr. and Mr. Buyer, how do I help you buy this house? How can we get to a number that makes sense for you so we can all make it work? Yes, I get a fee in the middle, because I brought this deal to the table."

Be proud of what you do as a wholesaler. You went out and found a deal and you need to get rewarded for that, because you too put in your time, money, and effort to find that deal.

Don't be dishonest. Don't be shifty. Don't be a used car salesperson (no offense to the good ones out there). Don't be someone who lies about what you're doing or gives half-truths. Just tell people the truth. "Listen, I'm going to put the house under contract, show it to all of my partners, and then decide what the best exit strategy is for us. Usually either me or one of my partners will close on it, and we will write 'and/or assigns' in the contract so that I have options and you have options, too. But, at the end of the day, Mr. and Mrs. Seller, you're going to get your money."

The same goes for when you find a buyer: Be open, honest, and prioritize great communication. Do this business with integrity, and you'll help ensure people don't view wholesalers and real estate investors as bottom-feeders. Instead, they'll understand that we provide a worthwhile service to people.

CHAPTER 6

HOME FLIPPING 101

The definition of a flip is simple: You buy a home with the intention to sell it as fast as you can, sometimes after doing a full renovation, sometimes after a quick renovation and cleanup, and sometimes after doing nothing at all! (Those are the best!) Typically, while doing a full renovation, it will take you three to four months to be totally closed with money in hand. The upside to flipping is that you can turn over many properties on an annual basis and create a lot of large chunks of cash. The downside is there is risk involved, and if you don't buy the flip right and manage the process like a boss, you can actually lose money. Here's something you may not know that will make you feel better: You don't need to do the construction yourself to make money—nor should you. As I shared previously, the first flip we ever did was a house that was very close to where we lived. At that time, Amber and I both thought that to make money, you had to do all the work yourself. We thought this because that's how most people think: You have to do all the work yourself to make all the money. But that's simply not the case.

So, we buckled up, went to Home Depot, and bought ourselves a bunch of tools and some cases to lug stuff around in the car. We thought we were hot stuff and went to work. The house needed new kitchen cabinets, a new countertop, some carpeting, a couple new windows, and a new paint job throughout. It basically needed some cosmetic work done and wasn't a lot of renovation, so we thought we could bang it out in no time.

Well, it turns out that if you're doing all the work yourself, it takes a whole lot longer—especially when you're not that talented. Amber and I didn't have a lot of skills—I didn't even know how to read a tape measure—but we knew we had to make money and we had to make it fast. Remember, when Amber and I started this business, we were $80,000 in credit card debt and had to get out; we had to find a way to make large chunks of money. The only way I thought I could do it was flipping. I didn't know about all the other ways you could flip; I just knew that the flipping you saw on TV was a way that you could get this done. So, we bought our first property using a bank mortgage for the house and credit cards for the renovation.

First, we had to clean the entire house. In the basement, we found an old furnace from the 1930s that was covered in asbestos, which we had to remove before somebody would even come take the furnace. I actually put on a full bodysuit, including goggles and a respirator, and had to spray the suit down piece by piece afterwards to keep myself safe. We did all that work ourselves, including putting in the kitchen cabinets and cutting out the opening for a new sink and putting it in, too. Outside, we put a new railing in, cut down some shrubs, and created an open porch out of an enclosed one. We used all our blood, sweat, and tears to get that renovation done. The only things we hired out were having the floors done and hiring one gentleman to come help us paint. At the end of the day, we purchased the house for $83,000 and put around $25,000 into it for renovations. When we sold the house, we made about a $17,000 profit.

The day before closing, we needed to prepare for a final walk-through of the house. When we arrived, there was about three inches of water in the basement—we'd had a horrible rainstorm and had no idea the basement had leaked. So, off we went to Home Depot to buy Shop-Vacs and multiple pumps. During the rainstorm, we were pumping water out into the yard because we had to get that basement dry before the buyer's walk-through the next day. We found two holes where the water was coming in, patched those up very solid, pumped all the water out, turned on the fans, and managed to get that house dry in time. We staged the house with all different types of clever details: one bedroom was too small to fit a king mattress in, so we took queen air mattress, put it on plastic milk crates, and put nice bedding on it. It looked great and like a full king-size bed—the only problem was it had a slow leak, and every day we had to go and re-pump the bed back up for showings. Ultimately, what we learned from this process was that you don't have to do all the work. As a matter of fact, it's far better if you use your time looking for good deals and then hire out *everything else*. When you do it this way, it can be done so much faster—and the holding also costs won't eat you alive.

FIND, FUND, FIX, FLIP, AND HOLD

Flipping really boils down to FFFFH: find, fund, fix, flip, and hold. First, you're going to buy a house, then you have to estimate the amount of repairs on that house. Next, you're going to hire contractors to get that work done. You can choose to have one main general contractor that subs everything out, or you can sub it out yourself—whatever you feel more comfortable doing. Remember, this process will require good management skills so you're able to stay on top of people and manage the entire process, as well as some visionary skills so you can see where that house is going to go.

There are four different kinds of flipping scenarios: 1. You buy the house and sell it as is. 2. You do cosmetic renovations, making the house look prettier or simply updating it. 3. You do a full renovation that may include major repairs. 4. You do a value-add flip, when you add on to the house to create more value when selling it. What makes all these different kinds of flips alike is you have to buy the house right. When you buy it right, that will leave enough meat on the bone—or enough money in the deal—for you to make a profit. Make sure you buy the home with enough room—financially speaking—because you're going to make mistakes in your first flips, and even on your tenth and twentieth ones. You're also going to want to have an *oops* factor figured in; prepare yourself for the fact that there are going to be unknown and unseen factors that come up.

Let me give you a real-life example. We once bought a house and did a full renovation flip, and when we finished and went to sell it, we discovered it was in a flood zone, so nobody would buy it. We then had to figure out a way to make that house profitable or get it out of the flood zone. Long story short, we got resourceful and figured out that we had to fill in the basement. If we got rid of the basement, that would change our elevation on the property and mean a different flood classification, meaning a cheaper flood zone—and *then* we could sell the house. We had to invest about $15,000 to get all that work done, though, because not only did we have to fill in the basement, we also had to move the furnace, electrical panel, and main water supply line upstairs. After we sold that house, we still made a $15,000 profit. We didn't lose money because we bought it right. If you buy low and sell high, you should always have enough money in between to cover whatever unexpected expenses crop up.

THE SILENT KILLER
OF REAL ESTATE DEALS

Remember, this process is also going to require holding costs. As long as you think you're going to hold a house, that house will cost you money. You're going to have to pay property taxes, school taxes, any HOA fees, electricity, gas, sewer utilities, and insurance on the house. These are all regular expenses that you'll incur as a result of owning the house. You're probably going to have some type of a mortgage payment, too. Every day that you hold the average $150,000 house, you spend about $100. You really need to make sure that you're managing your flip properly well so that you can minimize your holding days.

You don't pay most of these expenses every month, however. Many times, they are paid when you sell. You'll feel them when you sit down at the closing table and wonder why you made $5,000 less on a house. Chances are it's because you held it for three or four months too long. This is why holding costs are a huge part of managing the property. Therefore, if you budget to hold the house for four months, you better be in and out of the house in four months, because every month you hold that house, it's going to cost you another $3,000 or $4,000.

To minimize holding costs before you actually close on a house, obtain permission to go in and get all of your quotes and contractors lined up. Typically, this takes anywhere from two to three weeks or more to close on a property. During that time, get ahead of the game: have your contractors come in and start giving you quotes. Next, you'll want to put together a detailed scope of work that lays out exactly what you want to have done in every single room. This includes paint colors, skews, cabinets, the kitchen design, etc. The more detail you have in your scope of work, the less chance your contractor will make mistakes. It will also show the contractor that you're professional, know exactly what you're doing, and that they can feel confident working for you. Don't worry, we're going to go into more detail about managing renovations in a later chapter.

FOUR TYPES OF FLIPPING

1. Buy and Sell As Is

If you're fortunate enough, you might be able to find a house you can buy and sell as is. We once bought a house at an auction for $25,000 sight unseen—which I don't recommend unless you're incredibly familiar with the area—and never set foot in the house. Then we turned around and put it on the market for $65,000 and made about a $38,000 profit. These types of deals are home runs and don't come along every day. You have to be in the game to find them. You can't take the winning shot from the bench; you've got to be in the game and out there looking for deals all the time.

2. Cosmetic Renovation

I recommend doing a cosmetic renovation for your first flip. If it's going to require contractors, don't take on a full six-figure, $100,000-plus renovation. Instead, try and find something that's in the $30,000 to $50,000 range. Cosmetic means you're going to change some floors, do some painting throughout the house, maybe make some minor repairs, put in new kitchen cabinets, new bathrooms, new tubs, etc. Cosmetic flips aren't expensive to do, but they can change the entire look of a house. If you can get away from tearing down walls, that's best. But here's a pro tip: Whenever you can open up a house, buyers will open up their wallets. Therefore, if you can, try to open a kitchen up by taking down a wall between the kitchen and the living room, or the kitchen and dining room. However, if you do this, always make sure you have permits.

3. Full or Repair Renovation

Full or repair renovations typically occur when you have a bad foundation, there was a fire or a flood, if there's mold, or any other major problem with the house. These renovations are usually cosmetic plus any additional major repairs. Full or repair renovations also tend to be full of surprises, whereas cosmetic flips have minimal surprises. A full renovation, or a full gut rehab, is always going to have more risk involved, so beware.

4. Value Add

We covered this in Chapter 2, but as a refresher: A value-add flip is when you look at a home and determine that you can add something to increase its value. This can include adding more square footage, an extra bedroom, a second level to the house, finishing off a basement, etc.

You have to decide what type of flip is best for you based on your skills. What are you comfortable doing? What are you comfortable looking for? How do you identify an opportunity? For a renovation, it's all about the math, and you're going to have to get really good at a few things. One, you want to become an expert at finding off-market properties. Two, get really smart at estimating. Our Home Flipping Evaluator can really help you get a good, solid buy number that you can stick to—something that's especially important if you want to buy the house right.

COMPS

Next, it's time to run comps, or a comparable sale. You're going to have to do a guesstimate of what the house will sell for based on average comparable sales. Your comps should be houses that are very close by, on the same street or in the same neighborhood, that have the same school district, and are hopefully close to the same size and style of the house in question. The closer you can get to having all those things being in alignment, the better off you'll be. Once you have the prices of at least three solid comps—houses which have sold in the past six months and no longer—you'll have everything you need to make an intelligent decision. Now, it doesn't matter how much the house is. If you're in New York City or California, sometimes houses are $700,000,

$800,000, or $900,000. While the numbers may look scary, don't be afraid. If people are actually paying that for houses in the area and the comps show that, then it works. You can still use our formula no matter where you are in the country. It doesn't matter; math is math.

PRIVATE LENDERS

You now know what it's going to cost to repair the home, what you can offer to buy it, what it's going to cost to hold it, and what you can sell the house for. Then it all just becomes a math equation. If it's a great opportunity after you've put those numbers together, then put the deal together. How do you find investors for flipping? Once you find a deal, you'll find private lenders to fund those deals. In other words, once you have a deal, the money will come, because now you can go to those investors you sent those packets to and say, "Hey Grandpa, hey John, hey Dad, hey Uncle Bill, remember I sent you that packet? Well, I actually have a solid deal now and here's what it looks like. Here are the pictures, here's my return, and here's what you'll make, because I'm going to borrow the money for about four to six months. I'd love to have you as an investor. What do you think? Are you interested, or do you know anybody that would do this?"

STAGING

There are different kinds of staging: no staging, basic staging, and full staging. No staging is self-explanatory, and basic staging is when you simply put some curtain rods and curtains around the house. Maybe you add some color, put hand towels in the bathrooms, or add a couple decorative pillows around the house. Don't bother putting in beds and other furniture; just splash some color around so the house looks better. On the kitchen counter, you might put a few knickknacks and a couple signs around that say "Home," "Love," and "Family," to make it a little bit generically homey.

A full stage is when you rent furniture from a local furniture house, they bring it in, and you deck out every single room—including all the cosmetic stuff—and really make it look like the house has been lived in. In a hot market, full staging isn't necessary, but it really works in a slow market or if you're in a very high-end market. You want to have whatever the buyers are expecting for that size house in that neighborhood. Once you're done staging, then it's time to list the house.

REALTORS

Once you have an actual deal in your hand, people can look at something they can really sink their teeth into. When you're done, I'm going to recommend that you list it with a local real estate agent, unless you're an agent yourself. When Amber and I started our first flip, I tried to do it for sale by owner (FSBO), and despite getting a few nibbles, I didn't really know how to do it, how the process worked, and wasn't sure what paperwork I needed. I tried to put that deal together and was unable to, so finally, after three or four weeks of trying on our own, we hired a realtor. It cost us 5 percent to have the realtor come out, and he sold the house in three weeks—and that was in 2008, when the market was really tanking. He was successful because he had access to buyers and was able to handle all of the negotiations. This is why I recommend you list the house with a realtor when you are done.

DOS AND DON'TS OF FLIPPING

Don't buy with emotion. Sometimes people get so excited about buying a house that they quickly fall in love with the house—don't make this mistake! Fall in love with the *numbers*, instead. There's no room for emotional decisions when flipping houses.

Don't use eraser math! This is when you start to change the numbers on your Home Flipping Evaluator to make the numbers work, even though you know they don't add up. For instance, you want to buy a house and the numbers are off by $3,000, so you start to change your estimates thinking you can buy used materials, or do some of the work yourself, or cash in on that favor an old friend owes you to get some painting done, etc. Be careful, though, because if these ideas don't work, you are right back to the actual numbers, so don't use eraser math, use *real* math.

Don't design a house how you would like it. Instead, design the house generically with neutral colors—nothing too bold or too bright. Just because you like something doesn't mean the rest of the world's going to like it. Remember to always look at the home through the eyes of a first-time home buyer, if that's the target market you're going after. Amber and I spent a lot of our early years going after this demographic, so we kept purposely our prices around $150,000 to $200,000 because we knew that first-time home buyers weren't expecting to spend a lot for their first house, nor were they expecting much from it. Ultimately, you have to know who your buyer is and who you're going to tailor the home to. Just make sure that your design appeals to the majority of people out there. If you're not sure what to do, look at the comps. What are typical colors of the houses people are buying right now? What's the typical style in the kitchen that seems to be pulling top dollar? Do all the houses have an office in that area? Is that something you have to make sure that it has, too? How are the bedrooms designed? What is the master bath like? Does it have a walk-in shower or overhead showers? Since we have the luxury of having the internet right there at our fingertips, we can do a simple search and find out what houses that have sold for top dollar in the past year look like. Keep these things in mind, but don't spend a lot of money to make the house look amazing.

Don't ever hide anything. We never go looking for problems with a house, but if we find one, we deal with it. If we open a wall and we see some rotten wood, we don't just cover it up with a piece of Sheetrock and keep going—that will definitely come back to get you! We believe what goes around comes around, and if someone finds something later on and thinks you hid it, they can sue you. So if you see something bad in the house, fix it right away.

Do always make sure that you get permits on your work. We once had a woman who bought a flipped house from us that had a leaky roof who kept blaming us, and we kept telling her that she had an odd-style roof on her house. It was a barn-style roof, and despite it being brand new, the way it was designed, it collected ice all the time. Eventually, the water would back up and it would continually leak into the house. No matter what we did, she kept saying, "Well, you guys didn't do the right thing." Because we had the correct permits, however, we went back to her with all of our documentation. We even tried to help her and fix it for free. This woman eventually called the Better Business Bureau, so we gave them all of our permits, contractor estimates, invoices, and everything we had done after the fact when we tried to make things right with her, even though it wasn't our fault. After that proof, the matter went away. Thank God we had it! Another reason you should always get your permits when doing a renovation is because if a building inspector comes by and sees you're doing work without a permit, you'll get blackballed and they can make it very difficult to do work in your neighborhood.

At the end of the day, home flipping is how you earn those big sums of cash—you can make $50,000, $60,000, $100,000, or even $200,000 for flipping a house. Wholesaling can make you a good chunk of money, there's no risk in it, and you don't use your own money. While there is more responsibility involved when it comes to flipping, your profit margins can be much greater, too. Depending on what you want to do and what your financial goals are, you'll be able to decide which path is the best for you. But the better you manage that flip all the way through, the more money you're going to make.

CHAPTER 7

MANAGING
LONG-TERM RENTALS
(WITHOUT BEING A LANDLORD)

Before Amber and I became famous for flipping houses back in 2007, we bought our first rental property in 2005. Amber was still living in Texas, I was in New York, and we were business partners in another venture when we decided we were going to buy a property in upstate New York. I went, took a look, and was so desperate to buy a property that I bought it purely on emotion. I forced a deal where there should have never been one. We bought a house that had everything wrong with it. I had professionals and my friends go look at it. A home inspector even said, "I wouldn't buy this." My best friend, an experienced contractor, told me he wouldn't touch the house with a ten-foot pole. But I liked the math on the house, so I thought it might work. I didn't care about anything else; I just wanted to get into the real estate business and make a purchase. Do not make this mistake yourself, though, because I'll tell you, it's a *very* costly mistake.

So we bought the house and I became a landlord—what a terrible experience that was. We had tenants who knew how to work the system. The ones upstairs would pay their rent, although I had to chase it down and they'd usually break it up into two or three payments throughout the month. The downstairs tenant would often not pay at all and come up with some kind of excuse. What we were told during the inspection process was that the previous owner had cobbled everything together—he never called professionals to fix anything. Therefore, everything from the plumbing and the electrical to the structure was botched. In fact, he had taken out load-bearing walls so that the house was literally about to fall down, but it looked okay on the outside because it had siding that covered a lot of mistakes.

After we bought the house, we had nothing but problems when we managed the property. Every time there was an issue, one tenant said he wasn't going to pay the rent until we fixed it. It finally got so bad that he would call the building inspector, who, thankfully, we knew. The inspector told me, "I know how this works; they'll call me when they want something fixed, but when they don't want to pay rent, they will call me to come over." That's the leverage they had on us as a tenant. I was a landlord who was learning how to hate being a landlord. I didn't *want* to be a landlord; I couldn't manage the property well and I was starting to think it was a bad investment. Eventually, after not having paid rent for several months, the situation got so bad that we had to evict that tenant. At that time, the building actually became vacant. We managed to keep that property and made a couple dollars a month, but it wasn't worth my time and effort.

Looking back now, I can see the red flags: besides all the things wrong with the house itself, it had massive location problems. It was directly on a very busy road, and therefore covered in street dirt. It was also across the street from a chemical plant and right next to a bar that was called the Bad Pig (which was owned by a cop that got thrown off the force). Right down the street was a dump, and on the other side of the Bad Pig were loud railroad tracks that led right into the chemical plant. It had everything wrong with it, and six months after we bought the house, one of the neighbors told us that sadly, someone had hanged himself in our garage before we owned it. In other words, this house had everything that could possibly go wrong, *go wrong*. Every sign pointed to no, but the emotional side of me had just wanted to get into real estate. That's why I forced the issue when I bought the house and then ended up having massive tenant problems for several years, ending in eviction. On top of that, they damaged the house, which was already in very rough shape.

How did we finally turn this deal around? Many years later, we used private investor money and invested well over $100,000 dollars to completely renovate the house. It went from a house we paid $120,000 for to two really nice apartments, one upstairs and one downstairs. By putting money into it and dramatically repairing the property, we got a new appraisal for $230,000, so we were able to at least get money back into the property. Eventually, we started to have better tenants and charged more rent, going from getting $700 to $800 per unit to $1,200 to $1,500. This house was the first one that we owned, and guess what? We still have it to this day, and probably will for many years to come.

WHY LONG-TERM RENTALS?

Long-term rentals can outplay the stock market because real estate will beat inflation every day of the week. Real estate keeps pace with inflation, because it appreciates—and it has appreciated for over a hundred years, consistently. There might be some pockets where the market goes up and down, but overall, it has always appreciated in value. Plus, you get tremendous tax deductions for being a property owner.

Long-term holds in real estate are how most people have traditionally invested. You buy a property, fix it up if you need to, and then rent it to good-paying customers for at least a year, but optimally for three to five years, so that it pays a nice solid 10 to 20 percent return. With the explosion of the flipping, wholesaling, and short-term rental markets, long-term rentals have been overshadowed. But make no mistake: Rentals are the real key to building your wealth. It's money every month, and once you pay it off, it's a huge asset. It's asset-based cash flow and already keeps up with inflation, which also makes it a great retirement option. Everyone should have long-term rentals as part of their real estate investment portfolio. They're safe, clean, and relatively low-maintenance. They also create steady and predictable cash flow and allow you to pay your mortgage as you build equity in the properties that not only create wealth, but also create equity to invest in other areas. And it is a totally hands-off investment if set up correctly. You will *not* be the person who is fixing the toilet in the middle of the night. We have all heard those horror stories, but they do not need to be your reality. Smart investors know how to set it up as a hands-off investment they can be proud of, not one that sucks all your time and energy.

At our Home Flipping Workshops, we show our students in a step-by-step presentation how to build real wealth in real estate rentals without using any of your own money. It blows everyone's mind. Let me do my best to simplify it for you here.

Use private money or hard money (not yours) to buy a house that needs only a little work. Fix it up as a rental, then put a tenant in the house. Go to your local portfolio lender (a local lender who does not sell off your loan). They will give you up to 80 percent LTV (Loan to Value) as a loan on the house. If you bought it right, you should be able to pay off your private lender, plus put a few thousand or more in your pocket, tax free. Why? Because it is a loan, not income. Now, do this one time a year for ten years, and stop at year ten. Then use all your rent to pay down the mortgages.

This simple side hustle can create two things. In about seventeen years, you will own ten houses, free and clear, all paying you rent. This would be over $100,000 a year in passive income. But here is the hidden treasure: Your houses will not only pay you money like an ATM each month, but ten houses will be worth millions! And they are all yours! What if you did a few houses a year for the next ten years? Imagine the cash flow and wealth this creates for your family for generations. And the best part? When you are no longer here, rents continue to come into your family. This is the most powerful retirement strategy I know.

PROPERTY MANAGERS

Hire a property management company to look after your properties—*do not* do it yourself. When looking for a property manager, know that they'll charge anywhere from eight to 10 percent of the rent to manage it for you. They take the middle-of-the-night phone calls, they deal with tenants that have to be evicted, and they find and put in new tenants. I used to walk or drive by three or four houses every day, and people would wave to me and have no idea I was their landlord. They had no idea Amber and I owned the property, and I liked it that way. Our kids went to school together and I didn't want them to know that I was their landlord. I prefer to stay anonymous and just know that they're paying their rent, I'm paying the mortgage, and I'm also building wealth through the process.

TURNKEY PROVIDERS

If for some reason you don't have good deals in your area, there are plenty of places around the world where you can find them, and plenty of people called turnkey providers that can help. These people will actually sell you houses that they have just renovated and flipped. They actually sell them to landlords, fully occupied with a tenant and producing money. One of my friends calls every house he has from such an arrangement his own ATM, because it spits out money every single month. Therefore, if you don't want to do all the work yourself, you can actually go to a turnkey provider and let them buy the houses for you, and you can even finance those.

CASH-ON-CASH INVESTMENT

When you're inside real estate investing, you're looking for a few things. First up: What is your cash-on-cash investment? For instance, if you had to put $10,000 down on a house, and the return you got was $500 a month in positive cash flow, that's a 60 percent cash-on-cash rate of return. (Pro tip: Always remember to think about the value and power of being able to leverage other people's money to do this.) Look at how much cash you're putting into the deal, as opposed to what your actual return is—that doesn't even include the appreciation of the property itself. As the property appreciates, you get more and more value on the house, along with your cash flow increasing. As you're paying down debt, as you're paying down your mortgage, you're also getting more equity. In other words, when you owe less on the property, that becomes equity to you, *plus* the property is going up in value.

MULTI-FAMILY INVESTING

You'll always get better cash flow with multi-families, and here's the rule: The more units you have, the more work they are, but the more money they make. When you have one to four units, that's still considered residential, and you'll be able to get mortgages and use lending. Anything over four units is considered multi-family, and therefore a commercial investment. Any multi-unit will always garner more cash flow than a single-family for one main reason. When a single-family house is vacant, there's no money coming in at all. However, it's very rare for all units in a multi-family to be vacant at the same time. So, even though you may not have enough money to cover all of your expenses in a given month, in a multi-family, the odds are you'll still have a good chunk of money coming in, because at least one unit stays rented. The more units, the more positive cash flow.

Off-market, multi-family deals will provide you with instant equity. If you negotiate right when you're buying a house, you'll have instant equity in the home. This is true for multi-family, too. If you buy a multi-family unit off-market, you can pick up $50,000 or more just by buying the property off-market. How do you identify a great opportunity? Again, it comes down to math. Use our evaluator so that you know after all the expenses every month—like maintenance costs, repair costs, and vacancy factors—you're still making positive cash flow, paying down your mortgage, and getting equity in a property. Then you know for sure it's a great investment. Ultimately, a good rule of thumb is 1 percent: if a property is $100,000 and you can rent that house for $1,000—or 1 percent of the purchase price—typically that's going to be a good deal. This doesn't always work out, but it's a good way to see if you're in the right ballpark with a property.

There are also many ways you can structure multi-family deals. You can do long-term rentals in which you own the property and rent it out, which is what Amber and I do. You can also do lease options on properties in which you buy the house, fix it, and then sell it on a lease option. This means you retain ownership of the home yourself, or your entity does, but you lease it to somebody else with the option to buy. The idea is they give you $5,000 or $10,000 as a down payment on the house, then they pay more for rent and take care of all the maintenance on the house themselves. They could even pay the taxes if you wanted them to; that's going to be up to you. It's fully negotiable how you want to set that up, but the better the tenant, the better they'll take care of your property. Now keep in mind that a very low percentage of people who enter into lease options actually end up buying your house. So, if you end up getting a tenant who gives you a large down payment and more of a down payment every time that their lease option expires in a year or two, and they're paying you a monthly fee, that's more money for you, and they're also going to take better care of their property. Why? Because they actually believe it's their home.

DOS AND DON'TS
OF LONG-TERM RENTALS

Don't do eraser math and kid yourself on the numbers. You don't want to get into a situation where you are losing money every month, but you don't realize it until something happens and you don't have the money set aside to deal with it.

Don't expect your tenants to take care of your property as you would. We have a property that I used to drive by every day and see the tenant was parked on the front lawn. During the springtime, it was getting muddy and I saw tire tracks in the yard. I used to call my property management company and ask them to get them off the lawn. Finally, after this happened multiple times, my property management company said, "Glenn, I want you to know that they pay their rent on time without question, every month. We don't have any hassles, any headaches, we don't have any maintenance problems with them. They do park on the lawn, because they're trying to fit all the vehicles for the people that live in the home. But they don't smoke in the home, they don't have any pets, and I just want to tell you: it's just grass. We can put grass seed and dirt back on that and fix that one if they move out." After this, I just let it go because I realized it *was* just grass and I could fix it. If they're paying their rent, that's all I care about. And you know what? Those tenants are still my tenants to this day.

Do always hire a property management company.

Do abide by local laws. Protect yourself by always making sure you abide by them when it comes to your tenants. However, make sure that you screen your tenants as best you can. If you're allowed credit checks, do them, and get a good security deposit down, as well.

Do or Don't allow pets. You can choose to allow pets or not. We have allowed pets because we found that we can get more money for them (tenants have to pay extra each month for pets). However, some pets will do damage. If they start peeing and pooping on the floor, it's not only disgusting; it can actually ruin your house. Just be careful.

Do annual checks on your property. Have a clause in your lease that says you can check on your property and see how it's doing on a yearly basis.

Remember, not everybody lives as neat as you do. Some people live a lot messier, but how is your house doing overall? Go in, check, and make sure things are okay. This helps ensure you're giving people a nice, clean, safe place to live.

CHAPTER 8

THE EXPLOSION OF SHORT-TERM RENTALS

While long-term rentals can make you a few hundred dollars a month per property, short-term rentals can make you $1,000 or $2,000 or even more in positive cash flow per property. What if you could come up with five properties in the next five months and add $10,000 a month to your cash flow? What could that do for your life? Well, that's not usually possible with traditional rentals, but it *is* possible with short-term rentals.

Let me first tell you about our short-term rental story. Three months before COVID hit, Amber and I bought the house across the street from us in Upstate New York. It was a beautiful, Cape Cod-style, four bedroom, two bath on nine acres of land. When we bought it, my plan was to turn it into a long-term rental because that's all I did. Then we got to thinking about short-term rentals and wondered, "Gosh, could that work?" Then I said to myself, "Who in their right mind wants to go to Rotterdam, New York, on vacation?" But then I opened up my mind a little more and realized that there are people that travel to these cities for a variety of different reasons. Therefore, I decided to try it and see if it worked. So we renovated the house, furnished it, and put it on Airbnb.

Now, Airbnb is just a platform that connects homeowners with traveling guests. There are other short-term sites like VRBO and many more that all connect property owners with guests who want to rent their homes out. They can rent your home for a day, a week, a month, or multiple months, but you get to charge *per night*—and charge a lot more than you would for a regular tenant. It's almost like being a hotel owner in a lot of ways, because you have guests, not tenants. Platforms like Airbnb, VRBO, etc. provide you with a website and app to manage your properties. They drive in the guests, and you take it from there. You can manage who you want at your property. We do this based on their previous reviews and experience as a guest in other short-term rentals. You can also oversee all communication with them, provide door access, your house rules, and so much more. These platforms have literally created a new category in the rental space.

When we decided to give this a try, everybody thought we were crazy—but that's normal. Everything we do, people think we're crazy until it works; then they think we're brilliant. So we opened an Airbnb in Rotterdam, Upstate New York. We put the house on the platform, and lo and behold, we started to get bookings—and then we started to get *more* bookings. And then it started to book up on a regular basis.

Remember, we lived across the street; nobody knew we were the owners, but we watched people come and go. Some were traveling for work, including a work crew that came in to work on the local IT lines, and a performing group of actors and dancers. We found that families traveled to town for funerals, graduations, birthday parties, and sometimes just to get away. And all of a sudden, we discovered that if it stayed rented on a short-term basis, we would start to make $4,000 to $5,000 a month in rent. Had we rented it long-term, however, we only would have made about $1,500 to $1,600 a month. Now, we were pulling in more than twice that on the same property. Our eyes were opened to an entirely new experience.

And then COVID hit. At first we thought, "Uh-oh," assuming lockdown and social distancing guidelines would limit traveling. But we soon realized that, *because* of the pandemic, people from other areas like New York City wanted to get away from the city and come up to the country. We had a family stay there for three months and they paid $3,500 per month in advance on Airbnb. The platform charged us a rate of about 3 percent for that booking, but it also provided insurance, so it was well worth it. We couldn't evict tenants from our long-term rentals in New York during COVID, but as soon as tenants would move out, we started to convert those properties over to short-term rentals. What a blessing that has been—we've seen our numbers skyrocket from a few hundred dollars a month to a couple thousand dollars a month, per unit. Just in the past two years alone, we've purchased and converted thirteen short-term rentals. Those thirteen units outperform fifty others; they bring in somewhere around $50,000 per month in gross rent.

THE PERKS

Airbnb has completely changed the game because they introduced a new disruptor to the market. There's a reason why the company is worth billions and billions of dollars—they changed the market and allowed people like us to make massive cash flow by renting our houses out and letting the app do the work for us. Amber has been building this portfolio—it's her baby—and our son Dakota, who is twenty-two years old, manages these properties from his phone.

The difference between short-term and long-term rentals—in addition to the cash flow—is that your house isn't getting destroyed by long-term tenants. When tenants stay in a house for a year, two years, three years, or more—day after day, night after night, experience after experience—there's going to be natural wear and tear on a house. When a guest is only there for a couple nights, however, there's not a lot of wear and tear. We don't allow pets in our properties in our short-term rentals, so there's no pet damage, and guests simply aren't there long enough for this to be much of an issue. A lot of times our guests are on vacation, meaning they're doing something else during the day, and your property is just a place to sleep.

What's more, we don't have to evict anybody—that's a beauty. This is because short-term rentals have guests, not tenants with a lease. Additionally, the house gets cleaned on a regular basis. The guest also pays the cleaning fee, which is about $125. This means we have eyes inside the home constantly, looking around to make sure everything's okay. Ultimately, there are a lot of benefits to doing short-term rentals, including cash flow and the protection of your property. It's an amazing process if you know what you're doing.

FINDING SHORT-TERM RENTAL PROPERTIES

While there's no exact science on how to identify a great opportunity for a rental, I will tell you this: Any place where there is a hotel nearby, odds are there are travelers coming into town. This means you can have a short-term rental, as long as it's legal in the area. (Note: it's not legal in *all* areas, which can be a challenge.) Especially after COVID, a lot of people don't like to be in hotels and around a lot of people; they prefer to be in small family settings. For my family and I, every time we travel, we stay in Airbnbs and VRBOs. That's because our family is too big for a hotel. When we all travel together—including ourselves, our kids, and our nanny—we have seven people. We would have to get three hotel rooms to fit us all, which would be very expensive, or we can just rent an Airbnb for a fraction of that cost and feel like we're home away from home.

You can do short-term rentals almost anywhere, including apartment buildings and even remote locations. When researching properties or houses that you want to turn one into a short-term rental, there's a great service called AirDNA. It goes over what things rent for, what the dynamic pricing should be in your area, what you should charge for rooms, what you can expect to make, as well as information about the property, the area travelers, nearby restaurants, and more.

If you don't have the cash to purchase a short-term rental, you can arbitrage it. You can lease an apartment or house and then turn it into a short-term rental for yourself. As long as the landlord approves and you have the right paperwork, you could actually run a short-term rental on a property you don't even own, creating cash flow out of nothing.

WHAT YOU'LL NEED AT THE PROPERTY

First and foremost, you'll have to furnish the property and think about all the things somebody needs when they travel. You'll want kitchen supplies, including glasses and plates and silverware, a coffee maker, appliances, a microwave, a blender, etc. When it comes to linens, you'll want to invest in two sets of sheets and two sets of towels; that way, your cleaning crew can make the bed with one set of sheets while they're washing the other set. Pro tip: Have a washer and dryer in the house—it's a lifesaver. You'll also need the little things that people use regularly, like salt and pepper shakers, placemats, and toilet paper. For these things, you'll need a supply closet—and make sure you put a lock on it. Speaking of locks, you'll want to have remote locks that you can control from your phone, so you can let people in and out of the property, or you can give them individual codes. And don't forget the first thing all guests will look for: Wi-Fi.

Also note that if guests are going to pay you $300 or $400 a night, they're going to want some additional amenities. At the end of the day, you want to make sure they feel very much at home. When they come to any of our short-term rentals, we have a book that leads them in the right direction, telling them exactly where they can go for dinner, snacks, local stores—whatever they want.

FUNDING

If you're going to go the short-term route, you should treat it like a regular flip: You'll get regular investors, and once the property is up and making money, you'll use the bank to refinance, get your investor off that property, pull your cash back out, and move onto the next house. The only difference is you're going to have to make an additional investment to get the house decorated, set up, and ready to go with all the supplies, but with the extra income, that additional investment usually pays itself off in the first few months.

LOCAL LAWS

We've had our share of problems with local municipalities. Usually, if there's not a rule banning short-term rentals or limiting or wanting permits, there are some old-school-thinking people that don't like Airbnbs in their neighborhood. We've actually had two different towns call us after receiving complaints, and we've had to go in and defend short-term rentals.

We talked about all the pros and cons. The pros are that we're bringing people to the community, those people are spending money at local stores, and some of those people come to do house shopping and end up buying houses in the neighborhood itself.

Once we shared these things—on top of the fact that it's a revenue source for us—we had three different communities agree with us and let us continue our short-term rentals. However, I still have a backup plan, and always recommend real estate investors have a plan B and C just in case. If for some reason one of those towns says, "That's it. We're not going to allow short-term rentals anymore" (which I don't think they will), we'll just turn those properties into lease options—and I'll be able to get a good chunk of rent on them because those properties are all furnished. So, make sure you know the local laws before you go into a town, because some towns are very strict and don't allow short-term rentals, while others sit in a very gray area. Personally, if it's the latter, I'm going to at least go in there and *try*, and if they say I can't do it, then we'll go from there. Thankfully, most towns are realizing that short-term rentals aren't a bad thing as long as you keep parties out (more on this in a bit). If you manage your property well, don't allow parties, and keep good guests coming through the door—guests that aren't loud or getting drunk—then everyone can have a great experience.

PROPERTY MANAGERS

Don't manage the property yourself; be a business owner and let somebody else handle it for you. Depending on where you are in the country, there are management companies that will charge about 18 percent to manage your property. While you might think that sounds high, remember: They're dealing with people all month long. Sometimes they may even bring in more money because they use dynamic pricing. In other words, they're good at knowing when to lower prices and when to raise them higher.

MANAGING NEIGHBORS

Take care of your neighbors and let them know you're going to have a short-term rental. Also make sure you take care of maintenance on your property: mow the lawn, rake the leaves, and shovel the snow. You can even offer to take care of your neighbor's lawn—you're going to have a lawn guy there anyways. Spend the extra thirty dollars a week and have your neighbor's lawn taken care of. You can say something like, "Listen, I know it might be a little inconvenient for you. So what I'd like to do is go ahead and take care of your lawn for you. All I ask you to do is if you ever suspect something's out of line, shoot me a text." If you do a couple nice things like that for your neighbor, it might help keep them at bay and on your side.

PARTIES

We've learned a lot of ways to prevent parties from happening on our properties. One is to have an agreement with your guests up front, and to not allow instant bookings. Another is to make sure you see who the guest is and if they have previous reviews. If they don't, that means they probably set their account up that day. You want a guest who's been vetted by other hosts and didn't just create an account to look for a party house. If they're a local person that lives one town over, it's likely they're booking your house for a party. Since we live nearby, we let guests know that the owners live very close and are watching the property at all times. Another way to eliminate parties is to have a minimum two-night stay. There's also a decibel alarm device you can put in the house, so if a party is underway, it'll send an alarm to you so you know. If the sound is getting too loud, you can have cameras on the outside of the house to see what kind of cars are pulling into the driveway to keep an eye on your property. If there is a party and you have to ask a guest to leave, you can always negotiate reviews. When this happens, we say something like, "Listen, you guys have been too loud. We're going to ask you to leave." We don't leave them a bad review and they don't give us a bad one, either. We simply go our separate ways.

Ultimately, short-term rentals are an amazing way to build not only cash flow, but wealth. Amber and I like to buy the house and then put a short-term program in place, because then we get the best of both worlds: cash flow and appreciation. This differs from long-term rentals, in which you're getting a little bit of cash flow, but you're primarily in it for the appreciation as you pay down your mortgage. Imagine having short-term rental income and putting a whole chunk of that money you make every month into paying down that mortgage faster, and getting that house paid off in a fraction of the time. There's nothing more powerful than an asset that brings you tremendous cash flow—as well as appreciation and tax breaks. That's an investment that will make you wealthy beyond your wildest dreams.

CHAPTER 9

HOW TO NEGOTIATE

Negotiating is where you make your money. In fact, the most money you'll ever make per hour is when you're negotiating. For instance, you can negotiate with somebody on a house and drop the price $10,000 in a five-minute conversation—that's $10,000 for five minutes' work. It's a good idea to become an expert at negotiating. It's a skill that you're going to need in life, but the better you are at it in real estate investing, the more money you'll make. Remember, we make our money when we buy real estate, and that means we have to buy right, figuring out the most we can pay—or our Maximum Allowable Offer (MAO)—and still be profitable, and then going much lower than that.

I've said this once, but it bears repeating: If your first offer isn't embarrassing, it's not low enough. If your first offer doesn't make you squirm, make you uncomfortable, and give you sweaty palms, then it's not the right offer. You've got to go as low as you possibly can, because in negotiations, the people that are selling a house want to get as much as they can out of it, and the buyers want to buy it for as cheap as they can. That's true for anything in life—not just real estate. Anything that requires a negotiation, the buyers want to get it for cheaper and the sellers want to sell it for more. Somewhere in the middle is a happy medium—where you're both a little disappointed but happy—but as a buyer, you have to start low because you can always go up—but never down in negotiations.

If you determine that the MAO on a house is $75,000, or if that's the most you can pay for it, most of you might think your opening offer should be $70,000. I'll tell you that your opening offer should be between $30,000 or $40,000. Don't worry, there's a way to pull this off with negotiation, but you've got to get good at it. So how do you do this without making people feel insulted and having them hang up on you? Hopefully during the process, you've been a good listener. Every time the seller tells you what their problems are, you want to find out what need you can fill for them. It's not always money; it might be ease, simplicity, or speed, because they simply want to get out. Therefore, it's important that you listen to what they have to say. Don't always be talking. God gave us two ears and one mouth for a reason—because we should be listening more than we speak. This rings especially true in negotiations. It's more about listening and filling a need for the seller, and once you hear what that need is, use it in your negotiation.

For example, the seller might say, "I have to get this certain number, but I've got to be out in two weeks. I need my money in two weeks." You can listen to them, hear that, and try to make that possible. If they say, "What I really want is to not have my house torn up. I don't want to make this big house into apartments," maybe you can help them with that, too. If they say, "I don't know how to get rid of all this stuff in the house, I'm overwhelmed with all the things that were left behind," you can listen and then use that information during your negotiations to show that you can help them.

THE SELLER WHO WANTS TO GET OUT

Let's use the example of a seller who has a lot of stuff left behind in the home, maybe from old tenants or a parent who recently passed, and they want to get out fast. You've determined that your MAO is $75,000, so when you call them, you need to say something like this: "Hi, John. Listen, I'm working up the numbers and I'm not totally done yet, but I'm coming up with a number that's a lot less than I think you're going to want. I don't want you to be insulted by it. I just want to share the number with you and see what you're thinking. Again, I'm working the numbers and I'm a little uncomfortable right now, but I just want to share it with you. I know you wanted $75,000, and I have a few more estimates to get in to see and I could be off by a little bit, but it looks like I'm coming in around $45,000. Then be quiet. If they balk, then say, by the way, I can do everything you want. I can get the house closed in two weeks. Also, all that stuff in the house, you can leave it and I will deal with all the cleanup. We'll pay for all the closing costs and everything else. Like I said, we're going to make the process really simple for you and fast, because you mentioned that was important to you, and we can do that for you, but I'm coming in around $45,000."

Your tone of voice should be very concerned, like you're trying really hard to find a way to help them, because you are, but you also have to help yourself. Remember, you are the one about to take on the risk and relieve it from them. When you say the number, say it in a way that sounds like you're trying to do better, you're trying to get a good number, but you're just not sure. Once you say your number, stop talking and wait, because in negotiations, the person who talks first after an offer is thrown out is typically the one who loses. Then simply wait and see what they have to say.

Usually, one of three different scenarios is going to happen.

The Insulted Seller

One response might be, "There's absolutely no way that's going to happen." The seller might be insulted, to which you say, "Gosh, I really don't want you to feel insulted, but I do want to tell you where I'm coming in, just to make sure that you understand all the work that's involved and what I have to do." This gives you an opening to explain your price. Remember, you've not committed at this point; this style of negotiation doesn't commit you to anything. By saying, "I'm in the ballpark of..." you'll have room to maneuver. However, if they get mad, then you can say, "Okay, let me go back to the drawing board. I will do the best I can. Like I said, I'm not done yet. But let me ask you a question: Where do you need the offer to be? You know where I am, I know where you are, so where do I have to be so that you're happy?" And then list off all the things they want: "I can get you your money in two weeks. I can get the house all cleaned out. I'll also take care of all your closing costs to make it really easy for you. Knowing that I'll do all that for you, where do we have to be, price-wise?" You want them to give you a number of how low they're willing to go, because that's priceless information. Instead of shooting in the dark, you'll know exactly what number they expect. A lot of times they won't give you one, but if they do, that tends to be golden.

The "Is that the best you can do?" Seller

Another type of response you might get is, "That's a lot lower than I was thinking. Is that the best you can do?" Use the same answer as you would for an insulted seller. Say, "Well, I'm not totally done yet. I may be able to do a little better, but not a lot. Again, where do I need to be knowing that I'm going to do all this extra work for you?" Once again, you want to have them *give you* a number.

The "Yes" Seller

The other scenario is when a seller says, "Yes, I accept. That number works for me." If they tell you that on your first offer, I'm sorry to tell you, but you didn't go low enough. You actually left a lot of money on the table. They had a number in their mind and they were willing to go that low, but they were holding out to see what you'd say. If they were thinking they'd take $50,000 for the house, but you came in at $55,000, $65,000, or $75,000, then that's why they said, "Yeah, we'll take that" right away. That's when you know you went too high.

If a number doesn't work, at least you know what the seller's number is, and you can keep talking to them. As with many negotiations, the deal doesn't always happen right then and there. If you give a low number, you may not hear from the seller for a few days—or even weeks. But it's imperative that you stay in touch: shoot them a text, call them, or even send them a card saying, "Thank you for letting me be a part of this process." I've had my team bring people pies before, just to say, "Hey, we're thinking about you. When you're ready to sell your house, just let me know." Stay in touch with those people, because when they're ready to sell, they have to know they can call you. Sometimes they have to swallow that bitter pill, especially if it's a number they don't like. If you've ever had to pay more for something or take less than you wanted to, you know it took time to swallow that bad news.

In a competitive market, the seller also may go to somebody else. Stay in touch with them and say, "If something comes up, please let me know where you're at." Or you can even let them know to call you with any questions about the process. This way, you can at least find out what's happening. And remember, as much as you may want to negotiate, the sellers may be holding onto their guns on a number that just doesn't work. When this happens, you have to realize that you may not get every deal, and that's okay. As a matter of fact, it's better not to win some deals.

A REAL-LIFE EXAMPLE

We once looked at a house in a town called Scotia in New York and met with the owners. They wanted around $50,000 for the house, and it needed about $50,000 worth of work. It would be worth about $170,000 to $180,000 when we were done with it, but there's always risk when you're a real estate investor. Remember that you want to buy low enough so that you're covered, because you're the one taking on the risk. Don't forget to let the seller know this during negotiations. Say something like, "Listen, I'm taking over all your headaches. I'm taking over all the payments on the house. I'm taking over all the taxes, I'm taking over all the maintenance on the house, the lawn, the snow, the leaves. I'm taking on all the risk. So if I open that wall up and I find rotten wood, or a leak, or if my inspector tells me that the roof has to be replaced, that's on me. Please remember that I'm taking on all those risks, not you."

We ran our numbers through our Home Flipping Evaluator for the house in Scotia and realized we could probably pay $45,000 for it. Therefore, we decided to start our negotiations at $25,000— remember, they wanted $50,000. This is what we said when we called them:

> *"Jane, I appreciate you letting us walk through the house today. My wife and I worked up the numbers, and I wanted to call you because I'm not done yet, but I'm coming up with a number that's a lot less than what you wanted to get. I want to tell you why, and where I'm at, and just see if we're even in the same ballpark before we're*

close to being able to work something out. Is that okay, Jane? Can we do that? Great. So I looked at the house and there's a lot of stuff there. I noticed there might be asbestos, the roof needs to be replaced, and the furnace is near the end of its life. There were some things that I wasn't quite prepared for when I looked at the numbers, too. I'm still going through them and waiting for a few numbers to come in, so I'm not totally confirmed yet." (By the way, saying something like this is really important because it gives you an out.) "So I'm not totally confirming my number yet, but remember we're going to pay all your closing costs and take care of everything else, too. You just take whatever you want from the house and we'll deal with the rest, but I'm starting to circle around the number of $25,000."

Then I was quiet and waited. It was uncomfortable for about twenty-five seconds, and that twenty-five seconds felt like an hour and a half.

Finally, Jane said, "Well, that's a little lower than we were thinking."

"Can I ask you a question? What are you guys *really* thinking? Where do you need to be?"

"Could you guys come up to $27,000?"

Now, mind you, I was ready to go to $45,000, but I didn't accept right away. I said, "$27,000. Jane, can you hold on one minute? Let me ask my wife."

I put the phone down, looked at Amber, and said, "This is going to be a good deal." However, if I give, I want to get something from the negotiation, even if it's a small thing.

So I got back on the phone a minute later. "Jane, let me ask you something. If we agreed to $27,000, could we come back over and sign that paperwork tonight and get this deal rolling? Can we do it right away?"

"I don't see any reason why not," she replied.

"Okay, great."

Then we got in the car, drove over, and signed the deal.

We bought that house for $27,000, invested around $50,000 in the flip, and sold it for about $180,000. After all was said and done, we made $85,000. Now, had I paid full price, I would've made $50,000, but remember, we make our money when we buy, but we also take on all the risk. There could have been a problem with that house. I could have opened up the basement and found that one of the walls needed to be replaced, and that would've been a $10,000 error. Or I could've found a buried old tank in the yard, which would've cost me a few thousand dollars. There's always risk, but negotiation gives you room to protect yourself.

If you take anything away from this chapter, take away this: Your job is to see how low the seller will go. But remember, it's just a game, and—as with every game in life—there are rules.

1. Be a good listener.

2. Solve the seller's problems.

3. Be empathetic when giving your number, and don't stubbornly cling to a number.

Last but not least, don't confuse winning negotiations with getting a good deal. Those are two different things. Sometimes people get so wrapped up in wanting to win the negotiation that when they do win and get the house, they then realize they overpaid because they got so caught up in the process. This is why it's important that you stick to your numbers, be a great listener, and solve the seller's problems. Do that, and you can have a great deal. Remember: The most money you'll ever make per hour in the world is when you're negotiating, because you can trim off tens of thousands of dollars in one simple conversation. So get good at negotiating, because that's how you'll line your pockets in life.

CHAPTER 10

CLOSING 101

Closing is when all the legal transactions are complete, the title transfers from the seller's name to your name or the name of your entity, and the property is officially yours. There is closing on the buying side and on the selling side, as well as different kinds of closings when it comes to doing an assignment or a refinance. In this chapter, we'll talk about all of them. There are different strategies on how to close depending on the type of property you are investing in. Wholesaling, short-term and long-term rentals, and flips all have different intentions, different buyer and seller groups, and varied strategies based on the type of real estate investment. In addition, there can be many risks in closing, and you want to make sure you don't get left holding the bag, losing your deposit, or stuck in other potentially dangerous scenarios.

TYPES OF CLOSINGS BY STATE

First off, it's important that you know what type of a closing state you're in. There are primarily two different types of closing states.

Attorney States

In an attorney state, it is highly suggested or required that you use an attorney for all closings. This is what usually happens: Both the buyer and the seller have their own individual attorneys that represent them. Because they're attorneys, they tend to argue things out, and frankly, make the process much more expensive. Although attorneys at times can make closing much more complicated than it needs to be, the state may require their involvement, but in most attorney states, it is just accepted practice and not required (like they want you to believe). We like to use one attorney and have them do the entire transaction. Much easier and far less complicated!

Beware that crazy things can happen at closing, especially when you have the buyer and the seller at the same table, which is how it happens in attorney states. Sometimes, they'll even sit at the same table, and because there's so much money going around, sometimes there can be a lot of tension in the room.

People can tend to be a little squirrely and unreasonable. The very first house we ever bought, we were so nervous when we sat down at the closing table with the seller and her boyfriend. The boyfriend was kind of an old curmudgeon and decided that he was going to argue over $12.73 on the closing Statement of Sale (SOS), or HUD document. (The HUD document is what documents all the money at the transaction: who gets what, where it goes to, debits, credits, everything. This is what you usually use for your taxes at the end of the year.) Our attorney said, "I'm sorry, sir. That's not possible," and the boyfriend raised his voice. Then our attorney replied, "Sir, you will speak professionally in this office at all times." When the boyfriend raised his voice again, our attorney said, "I will not stand for that talk in this office," and then he walked out of the room. So there we were, sitting across the table from the seller and her boyfriend, in utter silence in the room for about forty seconds—which felt like four years. No one knew what to say, and I didn't want the deal to fall apart. Thankfully, Amber chipped in and said, "So are you guys excited to move?" which loosened the mood a little bit.

When anything unexpected arises, do yourself a favor: Stay calm. Remember, in any kind of an argument, the person that's out of control is usually the one with the problem. Don't let your emotions get the best of you. Remember: you want to lose the battle to win the war when it comes to closing. So, whatever the seller has to say, especially if they're upset about something, let your attorney handle it.

Title States

There are also what are called title states. This means closings for real estate transactions are done at the title company. There might be an attorney that's part of that title company, but both parties don't have their own representation. When it's done at a title company, you don't have as many problems because there aren't as many cooks in the kitchen.

You have to know which type of state you're in so you know where you'll be going for your closing, though. Typically, at this point in time, all closings are done in person unless you have special authorization or powers of attorney. Personally, we hope someday in the very near future that there will be enough security in place that closings can be done remotely, as that's the way most of the world is turning these days.

A WHOLESALE CLOSE

This is the most complicated kind of closing. Remember, there are two different types of wholesaling, so let's look at those now.

Assignment

An assignment of contract means that you never actually take title to the property, but everybody knows what you're going to make for an assignment fee and is okay with it. Let's say you put a house under contract for $50,000 and then you assign that contract to an end buyer for $60,000, making a $10,000 profit. You have to have that $10,000 labeled as an assignment fee. That way, at the closing table, the title company or the attorney's office will document that. The end buyer will bring the cash, the seller will get their agreed-upon price, and you will get your assignment fee.

Double Close

A double close is when you do an actual wholesale agreement, meaning you're going to take title to the property for a short amount of time. In other words, you'll sign the documents, take the title to the house for literally five minutes at the table, and then sell that property the same day. This means you'll be recorded at the county level and will usually show up in the local newspaper as owning that house for one day. If the assignment fee gets over $20,000, then, typically, to protect our interest in the property, we do a double close. Why? Because at a double close, the assignment fee is not public knowledge. So if you buy that house for $50,000 and you sell the house for $60,000, you're not the in-between person, but you're actually doing a double close—or buying and selling the property the same day.

At the closing table—whether it's an attorney's office or a title company—the buyer and the seller will usually be kept in different parts of the office. We make sure the buyer wires the money in the morning before the meeting or the day before. Once the funds are secured, then comes the signing of the paperwork, which can happen in a few different ways: everybody can come into the same place at the same time; they might be in different rooms in the title company; or the seller might come in the morning to sign the papers and get their money, and then the buyers come in in the afternoon to sign their documents and take ownership of the house.

The difference between a double close and an assignment is that a double close doesn't disclose all of the actual funds that are changing hands. This is in case you may not want to reveal the actual number you're taking home (because money makes people act funny sometimes). Most people are very happy with their deal at the time of agreeing to a price, but sometimes they don't like it when you're making more than they think you should make. If this ever happens, remind yourself: You are the investor, and you're the one that found the deal and made it happen. And at that time, everybody was happy with the numbers. So, don't let their greed get in the way of you being a successful investor.

There are a few states that are trying to outlaw assignment fees, and this may become more popular as time goes on. However, they can't outlaw double closing. Now, an assignment is less expensive when it comes to legal fees because you're not paying for two closings—you're only paying for one. But with a double close, you have to pay for both sides of the closing, both sets of filing fees, and all other closing costs that you would normally have to pay. While it's more expensive to do a double close, it might be worth it if you don't want to disclose the amount that you're making, or if you're in a state that doesn't allow assignment fees.

A BUYER'S CLOSE

When you buy a house—whether it's going to be a renovation, a buy and sell as is, a wholesale, or a rental—the closing process is the same. When you start it, the first thing they're going to do is do a title search, which will show you what liens are open on the property. At that time, they have to clear up any loans, and be prepared—unusual things can happen at closing. There may be a bank that went out of business or was sold three or four times back in 1995; maybe the people paid off the mortgage twenty years ago, but the bank never filed the papers to show that that mortgage was paid off. That means that before you can buy that house, you're going to have to get those liens cleared. Let your attorney or title company handle the details for you—that's what you pay them for. They will dig around and find that information, or they may allow that any of the unpaid liens to be covered under the title insurance that you're going to purchase. This will allow you to close.

Title Policies

Title companies write what's called a title policy or a title insurance policy as part of the closing. When you buy a house, you'll have a title insurance policy. That means that if any old claim to that property arises that was not found during a title search—maybe something from thirty years ago—and somebody stakes claim to your land from an old family dispute back in the 1950s, the insurance policy will cover that. Banks will also require you to get a title policy if you're working with a bank lender. If you're a cash buyer, you're not required to get a title policy, but I recommend that you talk with your attorney and see what's the best option for you.

If you're paying cash, there's also nobody looking over your shoulder to make sure the title search is done right. But if you're going to use a bank to buy that property, they're going to make sure that title is clean, because they're putting a mortgage on the property and want to be in first position. The bottom line is this: If you don't do a title search, you could buy a property for $50,000 that has a $100,000 lawsuit lien on it and have no idea, and then you'd be in trouble.

When you're doing a wholesale deal, it's not uncommon to find two or three liens from credit card companies or other problematic deals the previous sellers had. Maybe they had financial or bankruptcy problems and things got placed on their mortgage.

Whatever you find you can use as negotiating chips. As long as you all agree and the numbers work, those will get paid off at closing. In other words, once you give the seller their cash, it will be used to pay those liens off at the closing table, and they will get what's remaining.

If you're using a private lender of any kind, they're going to want to file a mortgage on that property, which someone will have to pay a fee for at the county. The note explains how much you're borrowing and what your terms are to pay it back. The mortgage is the legal document that secures the lender's investment to that property. This means that if you try to sell the property, or if someone tries to place a lien on that property, the lender usually is in first position. First position doesn't necessarily mean that they were the first one to file—some states will do it by what size the mortgage is, while others let you select. New York State, for example, is a race-to-file state, which means that no matter how small or large the mortgage is, whoever is the first to file is in first position. This means that if there's a default, they are the first ones to get paid. Therefore, if you're using private money, they're going to have a mortgage filed on that property so that if you default, they can take it back over. They'll have to foreclose on the property, but they can take that property back as collateral for the money they loaned you.

Insurance

Always get insurance on your property. If you have a lender, they're going to require you to have it and will usually name the lender as an additional insured. This protects their interest in the property, and they'll know if you default on your insurance payment. But always make sure you have insurance to protect yourself. It's a very minimal investment on your part to protect that asset. At the closing table, as soon as you take ownership, you'll have full insurance. Therefore, if something happens to that property—if it burns down or someone gets hurt—the insurance company will kick in and protect you for that.

A SELLER'S CLOSE

If a buyer comes to you with cash, then it's a very simple transaction. But if they come with a lender—which is what happens most of the time—there's a lot more paperwork you have to do. Sometimes during the closing process, it can be a bit of a pain because different parties may want additional information from you. For example, the closing company may say, "Oh, you flipped the house? Well, I want to make sure that you had the correct permits for the job." This is one of the many reasons you want to make sure you always get permits, because they're going to make sure you got them at the local level. This started in the past few years after so many flippers started cropping up. At closing, they started to require that you proved that you did the work legally and correctly. They may even ask for a scope of work that you did on the house.

If it's an FHA borrower—meaning a borrower that has an FHA loan, a VA loan, or another type of government-backed loan—they have certain requirements, too. An FHA loan buyer is usually someone who comes in and can put as little as 3 percent down. If it's a USDA loan, the buyer can do 0 percent down, and this sometimes applies to VA loans, as well. Then there's a conventional mortgage, which is usually 10 percent down. A conventional mortgage is a lot less strict, meaning there are fewer guidelines and you won't have to worry too much about flaking paint or anything minor like that. With an FHA loan, however, if there's any flaking paint anywhere—like even on an outside window or door—you'll have to paint that. They will not give the borrower a mortgage until that's painted. There are also certain spots where your property has to have certain kinds of railings, and at specific distances from one another. These aren't big things, but they can be annoying if you're not aware of them. If you want to get the loan to go through, make sure you take care of those small items that will satisfy the bank for an FHA loan.

Appraisals

When you're selling a house to an end buyer, part of the closing process is having an appraisal done. That appraisal will determine how much the buyer can borrow on the house. You can demand that they come up with cash for the difference, or they may just say, "No, that's what the house is worth, and that's what I'm going to pay you." Typically, the appraiser tries to come in right around the asking price to keep everything running smoothly—as long as it's within reason and they can prove it with the local comps.

If an FHA appraiser appraises your property and you don't like the appraisal amount—maybe it doesn't match up with what you think the house is worth or even what you sold it for—be aware that the FHA appraisal will still stay with the house for six months. That means even if you try to sell it to somebody else and they try to get an FHA mortgage, that amount still gets recorded. In other words, you can't really sell the house to somebody else who is using FHA financing just because the appraisal comes in low.

When it comes to cash transactions, they can take anywhere from forty-eight hours to twenty-one days to close. During COVID, it took up to forty-plus days now to close a cash transaction. Whereas, when you're dealing with someone who has a mortgage they're bringing to the table, that takes anywhere from forty-five to sixty days to close. This is because the banks have a lot of due diligence to do to make sure they can loan money on that property: They're going to need appraisals, to see inspection reports, and do a lot of due diligence on the buyer them-selves to make sure they have all their I's dotted and T's crossed.

We had a house for sale one time and were all ready to close. It took almost sixty days to get the closing done, and we were waiting for what's called a "clear to close." A clear to close means all paper-work has been done, all liens have been satisfied, and we are ready to do this official transaction and sign the papers. So while we were waiting for a clear to close, the buyer got laid off from his job *the day of* closing. That got leaked out at the closing table. He said, "I lost my job today," and the bank said,

"Whoa, lost your job. Never mind." They pulled out and didn't give him the loan, so we had to go find a new buyer. That can happen in these situations. It doesn't happen all the time, but you should be aware that it *can* happen.

How to Handle Problems at Closing

What happens if there's a problem at the closing table? Let's say a buyer walked through the house and determined that a window had been broken or the house had been vandalized. Now they want that window fixed and it's going to cost $500. The buyer can ask the seller to keep $500 or $1000 in escrow until it's taken care of. Or, if you have a situation where work that was supposed to be done in the house hasn't been completed yet—e.g., something wasn't finished or the final permit hasn't come in from the building department—the buyer may ask for that money to be held in escrow. This means that the attorney or the title company will hold that money until the situation has resolved itself. Whether they ask for a few hundred or a few thousand dollars, negotiate that amount, because oftentimes the money that goes into escrow is very difficult to get back out.

A REFINANCING CLOSE

During the rental chapter, we talked about how we use investor money to buy a rental property, fix the property up, increase its value, put a tenant in there, then refinance it to pull that cash back out. If we do it well, we can pull out free cash, too—more cash than we actually put into the property. To do that, you're going to use a bank. We recommend that for this type of closing, you use what's called a "portfolio lender," which typically isn't a large national bank, but a local bank that keeps their own portfolio of business and makes money by loaning money locally.

A portfolio lender has less strict terms, and using one is a great way to refinance your properties. If you do this correctly, you're going to refinance your houses in a company, LLC, or commercial name, and it becomes a commercial loan when you take it out in an LLC. What does that do for you? In most cases, that keeps those loans off of your personal credit report. All other mortgages that you get—for a personal residence, car, etc.—that goes on your credit report. But if you're a real estate investor and have houses closed and want to refinance them, those things won't show up on your credit if you refinance in a company name.

These closings usually take sixty days, and here's what happens: The bank or lender will do an appraisal on the property, they'll have a lot of paperwork they want you to sign, you'll have to negotiate your rate with them (you can usually shop around and find who wants to give the best rate and terms), and then you'll go to closing. You'll get your check at the closing table, provided there is money left after paying off the initial private lender, and the property's still yours, but now there's a loan on the property and you'll start paying the bank back for that.

CHAPTER 11

REHAB 101— THE KEY ELEMENTS

Every project you do is going to have some kind of rehab. Even a buy and sell as is for a quick flip is probably going to require some minor repairs. A rental will be a different kind of rehab than a full rehab, however, and then, of course, there's a full rehab. This is when you put in a new kitchen, new bathrooms, etc. There are three different ways you can get the rehab work done, which we'll explore over the following pages.

DIY

The DIY—or do-it-yourself—method always looks better on paper when you run the numbers, because it *looks* like you'll save yourself thousands of dollars—

if not tens of thousands of dollars—on not having to pay a contractor to do the work. The problem is, people forget that their time is worth money—and that their labor is worth something, too.

On the very first flip we ever did, we did all the work ourselves—I don't recommend that. At one point, I had to attach a sink under a kitchen cabinet. To do that, you have to be on your back in a very awkward position, reaching your arms up behind the sink cabinet to connect the plumbing to it. The opening of the cabinet is right in your lower back. Although I eventually got the sink connected, I tweaked my back in the process. When it flared up a few years later, it crippled me for almost ten months; I could hardly move. To this day, it's still an ongoing sore spot—one I can trace back to that moment when I was doing something I shouldn't have been doing. And there I was thinking I was saving money, but was I? Because it turns out it really cost me a lot of my own health. I know a lot of people who have done similar things while doing DIY construction or other work they shouldn't have been involved in directly.

There's another downside to doing all the work yourself, and that has to do with your time. Remember: You can't do multiple things at once. You can't tile the kitchen and the bathrooms while you're also painting and working on the backyard or the roof. Therefore, this DIY strategy drastically slows you down and eats away your time, and in real estate investing, time is money. Every day costs money. Therefore, although you may think you're saving money with a contractor, you're probably paying more than that with your own time investment.

Another thing to note is quality control. Some people are perfectionists and think if the job's going to be done right, they had better do it themselves, and so they overdo the house. They make it look amazing and worth a lot of money, but they take way too long and spend way too much money on it. They probably made the house much better than it had to be in order to get the same sale price, meaning they're not getting as much money out of that deal. I'm not saying do a cobbled-together flip, but you don't have to waste time, energy, and money overdoing a house when you can just do "enough" for a house.

If you're a perfectionist and can't relinquish control, you're going to drastically limit yourself on what kind of a real estate investor you can be. You've got to learn how to delegate in order to grow a real business.

Another DIY avenue is to live in a home for one or two years, and while you're living there, you work on the house. It's a very slow way to build wealth, but you can do it. You just need to ask yourself: Do you want to live like that? Do you want to be doing rehab and living in unfinished houses while you're flipping them? It's not the ideal living situation. But DIY is one way to flip a house—if you want to do one house a year and work crazy amounts of hours alongside your full-time job. It can be done, but the best use per dollar of your time will always be going out and looking for new deals. *That's* where your money's made. If you're busy tiling, working on plumbing, and doing electrical, you're not going to have time to go out and look for deals. If you have to wait until you finish your house to start the process, it will be very challenging for you to continue to be a real estate investor.

A Real-Life Example

In 2008 we had a house that we flipped in thirty-three days which made a $36,000 profit after renovating it ourselves. We were all-in during this time. In fact, Amber had to sell her car so we had enough money to finish this flip! For thirty-three days, about fifteen hours a day, we renovated—and we did not take one day off. Every day we made a list of what had to be done the next day, and we went room by room. We stayed focused on the goal, and whatever we didn't get done would move to the next day's list. At the end of the day, we got the job done, but we were exhausted. Not to mention, during that time we couldn't look for another house because we were so busy with our rehab every day.

Why did we do all that work ourselves? Because we thought that's what we had to do in order to make money. When we finally finished and had our open house, we were exhausted. The neighbors from across the street came and told us, "Do you know what you two have?" "No, ma'am. What do we have?" we replied. "You've got balls. You guys took a house during a time when people are afraid of real estate investing and have worked your asses off to be here."

We appreciated what she said, but we didn't have any grand vision—we were just trying to get out of debt. The ironic part is we had a bidding war and sold that house for $2,000 over our asking price when everybody was saying real estate was the worst investment ever. While it was hard work, it was worth it. But what we learned is we don't ever want to work that hard again, because there are other people that can do that kind of work faster and better. We realized that if we hired that work out, we could actually have a life while our business continued, which brings us to the next type of rehab.

HYBRID

A hybrid rehab is perfect if you're somebody who really loves doing specific types of renovation jobs—like tiling or electrical work—but not others. Maybe you're really skilled at painting, or your brother is an electrician and can do the job for next to nothing with your help. In a hybrid rehab, you handle the jobs you can do and hire out the rest. But whatever you do, don't kid yourself. Be well aware of the time it takes to work on even *one* aspect of a renovation—time you will spend *not* looking for your next deal. Remember: Every minute you spend on that job site is time you're not doing your number-one money-making activity.

A Real-Life Example

At the end of the day, hiring contractors for the job is the absolute best way to build wealth as a real estate investor. Just like you can use other people's money to build your real estate empire, you can also use other people's time—and they're professionals. That means they can do the job in a fraction of the time that you can do it, because they do it every day. They're not doing it part time alongside a job like you'd be doing it, which means they'll also get the job done better. The biggest challenge of doing renovations, however, is finding the *right* contractor. But, when you do, it's an absolute game changer because they'll go out and get the work done. Then you can spend time with your family, at home, growing your business, or doing hobbies. And you can look for your next real estate deal and not have to worry about the day-to-day minutiae of all the little nuts and bolts that have to be taken care of in a renovation.

Once we were working on a house and called in some contractor friends to give us an idea of what we should do. When we were cutting out the sink opening, our friend Bryan said, "Remember, you could always cut the hole bigger, but not too big, or you will ruin your entire countertop." It took us about five hours to cut the correct size opening for it, but we finally did it. We learned the same with the crown molding: a professional would have it done in thirty minutes, but it took us a lot longer because we weren't skilled in that area. Sometimes a hybrid becomes necessary when you just want to get the job done in an efficient way.

Our students were finishing up a flip recently and had a lot of spots in the house that needed to be touched up with paint. It was getting down to their deadline to finish the house, and the painter bought the wrong paint from Home Depot. They went through and touched up all the spots, trim, and molding, and when the paint dried, it was a different color. All of a sudden, in every single room in the entire house, there were different color splotches. At this point, the rehab became a hybrid because they needed to get it fixed and closed without having to hold the house for another ten days.

If you have a passion for some type of construction, if you enjoy it and get fulfillment from it, then do a hybrid, but let the other professionals do their part, too. That's the only way you can really be successful doing it this way. There have been many times over the years that I've asked Amber if she wanted me to hire out someone to do the design on the houses and she quickly said, "Absolutely not! I love doing design," so she does that part herself.

HIRING EVERYTHING OUT

At one point, we found ourselves in a situation where we were rehabbing two houses at the same time. All of a sudden, we realized it made much more sense to hire contractors to do the work because we couldn't be in two places at once. And, if you want to have two houses going at the same time, you're going to have to have multiple contractors. However, they can be tough to find, tough to work with, and tough to trust. But don't worry, we'll cover everything about contractors in the next chapter. For now, here are the different types of renovations you should be hiring out completely.

As Is Renovation

One of our students wanted to do a full flip on a house, but first it needed two major repairs: a new roof, because it was starting to leak, and a new furnace, because the old one had stopped working. Together, these two things cost about $10,000. The sellers couldn't afford to get them fixed, so they sold the house at a discount. We helped our students buy the house for about $154,000. They could have done a full renovation, but we encouraged them to only put a new roof on and a new furnace in it. Why?

Because it was the answer to the question: "How can you make the most amount of money on this project with the least amount of risk and time involved?" Putting on a new roof meant the new buyer could get a mortgage, so they paid $10,000 for the new roof and a new furnace—and that was it. We encouraged them not to do any more work in the house, because once you paint one room, the next room doesn't look good; once you paint the trim in one room, the next room doesn't look good; once you start renovating inside of a house, it gets very difficult to make it look good and not cobbled together.

We then suggested they put it on the market as is for $200,000, and they sold it in a bidding war for $205,000. With all the closing costs, commissions, holding costs, and everything else involved, they still netted approximately $30,000 for doing work that took about two weeks. They wanted to do a full renovation because they wanted to make it look pretty, but as an investor, you need to ask yourself: "How can I make the most amount of money the fastest?" which is really asking the question, "How can I make this house livable so someone else will want to buy it at a discount?" If they had made that house beautiful on the inside, they would've had to invest $50,000 in their renovations and two months' worth of time. The house would've been worth a little over $300,000, but they would have invested a lot more, with a lot more time—and a lot more risk. With the deal they took, they made $30,000 for two weeks of work, and remember, the faster you can get a renovation done, the more money you can make. That is how you make great money doing an as is renovation or flipping a home that needs very little repair.

Have a Plan B

On deals like this, we always tell our students to prepare a plan B. For example, if they put that house on the market for $200,000 and it didn't sell in the first two weeks, they would need to decide what their bottom line price was going to be. Were they willing to take a $25,000 or $20,000 profit on the house? Another option would be for them to go back in and do the full renovation—to put the other $50,000 into the house and put it back on the market for closer to $300,000, making a $50,000 or $60,000 profit. With any renovation, you should be asking yourself: What's the best way to get in and out of this deal? Every house is going to be different, and you have to make that decision based on the work that has to be done, how much time you have, and how long you want to hold that property.

Rental Renovation

When you do a rental renovation, it's the same as a full renovation but with a lot less work. You're going to consider painting kitchen cabinets and adding new hardware instead of putting new kitchen cabinets in. You might think about installing a laminate floor instead of a tile floor, or a laminate countertop instead of a granite countertop. Anything that's major that needs repair, since you want to use to the end of its life in a rental. For example, you may have a roof that has five years left in it. If you're going to flip that house, the end buyer on that flip is going to want to have a brand-new roof, but a tenant that's going to rent the house really doesn't care what the roof looks like. As long as it keeps them dry, they don't care. So you use that roof until you absolutely have to replace it. The same goes for the furnace. A buyer might want to have a new furnace, and you might have to install it in order to close the deal. However, if it's an older furnace and the inspector says it has five years of use left, you can maximize your return by using it until it stops working. Your bottom line on a rental flip is to make it a clean, safe place for your tenants to live, and that also applies for a short-term rental. Any major items that you don't have to repair or replace now can wait.

Full Renovation

When doing a full renovation, the first thing you want to have is a scope of work that details exactly what your contractors have to do. It's also important to be aware of what neighborhood you're in because you want to match the comps when creating your scope of work. Therefore, if other houses in your area have granite countertops, you'll need granite countertops; if they have tile backsplashes, you'll need a tile back-splash; if they have fancy lighting, you'll need fancy lighting. You don't need top-line appliances, unless you're in a neighborhood that requires that. You want to match the comps—but you don't want to overdo it.

Whether it's an as is, a rental, or a complete gut renovation, don't over-renovate. Over-renovating is the number-one reason why rookies lose money. Sure, you want your rehab to be a great place to live, but you don't have to go crazy, and you don't have to implement all of the fancy personal touches that you'd want in your own house. Regardless, if you're going to do a full reno, commit to a full renovation. Selling a house with half-done renovations is never a good thing, and it will tarnish your reputation. In summary, when doing a full renovation, you need to:

1. Do a full scope of work that details exactly what needs to be done

2. Manage the process (including hiring the contractor, getting insurance, managing all the subcontractors, and getting ready for the sales process)

3. Put it on the market and sell it

CHAPTER 12

BUILDING YOUR TEAM

To be successful in real estate—to be successful in any business really—you can only go so far by yourself. If you really want to grow and be a true real estate investor, you've got to have other people on the journey with you, which is why you need to become good at building a team. You don't want to be someone who tries to do everything yourself, because there are a lot of facets to being a real estate investor. Maybe you've heard the saying "Jack of all trades, master of none." You don't want to be a living example of this. Instead, you want to have a team full of masters who know what they're doing to make sure you're successful at what you're doing. A lot of money is at stake—and so is your future—so make sure you master building and managing your team, and then let everybody else master their own trade. That's how you build a successful real estate portfolio and real estate business, no matter how small or large. Because even if you're only doing one deal a year, you're going to need multiple people throughout the process. And remember: Not all of these specialists are created equal. You want to find people that are used to working with real estate investors because we speak a different language.

THE VALUE OF A TEAM

As you build a team, people whom you do business with on a regular basis will do work for you for next to nothing or for free sometimes, just to get you out of a bind. This past year, we moved from Upstate New York to Florida. The first day we moved we had red tide, which meant we had over 200 dead fish on our private beach. We had no idea what to do. In Upstate New York, we could call a number of people who would do this work for us because of the team we've built over the years. I could call them and pay them for the day to come clean up all these dead fish that were on our property—because it was getting hot and stinky and turning into a very bad situation. But that first day, we had to do it ourselves because we didn't know anybody in town yet. This really highlighted the value of having a network of people to me. The next time it happened, we found a contractor online who came out and cleaned up all the dead fish for us for $100. That was the best $100 we ever spent. The value of a team also becomes very apparent when you need something done and can just make a phone call, and because people work with you, they'll do it for you. That's the kind of team members that you want to find, so when you need something in a pinch, you can call them. That's the value of building a strong, solid team.

Dig Your Well Before You're Thirsty

You want to make these connections, have these contacts, and foster these relationships as soon as possible, so when you need them, they are there. Dig your well before you're thirsty. In other words, get all these relationships in place so that when the time comes, you're ready to pounce and not scrounging around looking for somebody under pressure. It's better to not call these people when you're in that state, because if you do, they'll charge you more because they'll sense your desperation. If you've already established a relationship and call and say,

"Hey, I got a deal I'm working. I need your help here," then the price will be right.

Keep these relationships strong, and keep all of your team members on your holiday card list. Check in with them, give them referrals, and build relationships with them. In order to have people who you can just call, you'll need time to build those relationships first, and build them with intention. Tell yourself, "I'm going to build a team of people so that when I need water, my well is full."

Take Back Your Time

Take back your time by not doing all the work yourself, and only do what you're good at or want to do and hire out the rest. Find people who are better than you in the areas where you're weak. A lot of us think doing the work ourselves is going to be cheaper, but they're not calculating how much time it'll actually take. If you are only working on the construction of the flip evenings and weekends, that'll take four to six months, meaning the holding costs end up costing you more. For a contractor, however, it might take only four to six weeks. Think about it this way: A property averages up to $2,000 to $3,000 a month in holding costs (more in higher areas), which means you're paying $75 to $100 a day just to hold a moderately-priced property. If I came and knocked on your door every day and told you to hand me $100, eventually you'd move a lot faster. That's why it's a silent killer—because you don't realize you're giving away $100 a day until it's too late. By leveraging other people, though, you'll gain more time and money because you'll have fewer holding costs. Plus, if you're scaling, you can't be in two places at once. The time that passes while the house is being renovated is when you need to be looking for your next deal. So save your wallet, your time, and your energy by hiring other people to do the work!

TEAM MEMBERS YOU NEED TO RUN YOUR BUSINESS

Let's dive into all the different team members you want to have, why it's important to have each, and how to find them.

Real Estate Agents and Referrals

You need to have people on your team who are always looking out for properties for you. You need real estate agents that can help you put together deals that you find on MLS. They know all the ins and outs, paperwork, legalities, and what you're supposed to do to get the deal done. They're going to be in front of your motivated sellers, so they can let you know about off-market deals. You'll also want to have referrers, which we talked about in Chapter 3. This includes people in estate sales, at junk removal companies, trash removal companies, and cleaning companies.

How do you find real estate agents and referrers? Through networking.

Brian and Tracy were two of our students that tried to sell their own house. They weren't real estate agents, but they wanted to save the 5 percent commission. Their house was a little over $200,000, meaning the commission was around $10,000. They tried for over four weeks in a hot market to sell the house and they were unable to. When they did finally get an offer, they weren't sure how to do the paperwork and put the deal together. It became a very confusing mess, and they actually lost that buyer. Between the extra holding costs and the lost buyer, they finally contacted a real estate agent. The agent put the home on MLS, and it sold within five days for $12,000 more than the asking price. Our students thought they were going to save money, but it actually cost them *more* money because they held the home for more time, and the real estate agent was able to get them above the asking price for their house and handle all the headaches for them.

Lenders

Whether you use family, friends, private lenders, hard-money lenders, or a home equity loan, you're going to need money that's readily accessible. That source of funds, which we covered in Chapter 4, will need to be part of your team.

Title Company or Attorney

A title company or an attorney will help you close the deal. They'll handle all the paperwork and legalities, and make sure all the I's are dotted and T's are crossed. This team member will protect you, make sure that you're buying a house with a clean title, and sees to it that the transaction goes smoothly. Obviously, you can try and do it yourself, but it would be a complete mess, and it's well worth the money to have them as part of your team.

Insurance Agent

You need a good insurance agent you can work with on a regular basis for your flips and rentals. This agent should understand your needs and goals—and can help you reach them. Remember, your agent should specialize in real estate, because traditional insurance agents probably don't know how to write policies for vacant houses.

Home Inspector

A good home inspector will have real-world experience, understand what you're doing, and not be an alarmist. You don't want someone who starts screaming and panicking every time they see black mold and scares you off of deals. You want them to be factual, to help you, and to be part of your team, who's already looking at houses with you on a regular basis. Of course, the better the home inspector, the more money you'll pay, but it's the best money you'll ever spend, ensuring you have a second or third set of eyes on that property. The right home inspector will also understand that you'll be looking at multiple houses and not just one house, because you won't be living in the house. You're going to renovate it and understand there are going to be problems, but you just want to make sure there's nothing really bad that you didn't see. This person may be a retired contractor or a current contractor, and should have at least eight to ten years of construction knowledge.

Contractors

There are general contractors, electricians, plumbers, septic and sewer contractors, cleaning contractors, HVAC, trim, Sheetrock, painting contractors, and more. When you're going through job sites, start to build out your team. See who you like and get their number directly if it's through a general contractor, and also make sure you know who to call in an emergency. Contractors are the most difficult to manage by far, but when you find a good one, take good care of them (and this goes for all your team members). Give them gifts, whether it's pizza at the job site or a case of beer when they go home on a Friday. Make sure that they know that you value them as a team member.

To find quality contractors, first ask for referrals, and make sure you're asking people who know how to work with real estate investors. You can find that at your local Real Estate Investing Association (REIA) groups. I also recommend going to Home Depot or any local supply store early in the morning to see who's coming in early to get their job started. You want to find people that are actually working. It makes me nervous in a hot market if we call a contractor and they're not busy. If a contractor's not busy and isn't booked out, that means they probably don't have the best reputation.

Similar to home inspectors, when working with a contractor, make sure they understand that you're a wholesale buyer. You're not somebody who's been saving for five years to get your kitchen redone so you're likely to be high-strung; you're going to make the process easy for them. It's going to be a vacant house, you're going to give them a scope of work, and they won't have to go out and do a lot of estimates or any marketing. Your ideal relationship will be when you call them and say, "Here's my next property. Here's my scope of work. Can you meet this budget?" and they go in and do it. Now, not every contractor wants to work with a real estate investor, so you have to find the ones who do. Some are flippers themselves and just want to do deals in between their own flips, and that's okay, too.

Lastly, make sure your contractor has all the right types of insurance in place, including liability insurance, workman's comp insurance, a contract, and whatever else you need in your local area to ensure that everyone is protected.

Suppliers

We do a lot of our work with Home Depot because they take great care of us. In fact, we're one of the largest buyers in the country, so we're able to pass that discount onto our students. They're kind of a one-stop shop for almost everything, and that makes any job go faster. Remember: The faster the job goes, the more money you make.

Designer

You're going to need a designer. If we didn't have Amber, we would have to hire one. Some people have vision, and some people don't. It's as simple as that. When we walk into houses together, I would see the money crystal clear, including what we would have to pay for it and how much the repairs would cost, within $1,000. As a designer, Amber can always see the vision for the property. She'll walk into this ugly house and say, "I can make this work," and turn something ugly into something beautiful (I always tell her that's why she's married to me). But if you don't have a designer as a part of your partnership, you're going to have to find one.

Code Enforcement Agents

You want to have code enforcement for your local municipality on your team. How? Go to them and ask them questions like: What do you need in this area? What kind of permits do I have to have? If you show you are trying to do things the right way and not avoiding or skirting around them, you'll have a good relationship with them. Then, if you get busy and they can't make it out in time, you can simply take pictures of a house and sometimes they will let it slide.

Many years ago, we were in the middle of a renovation, and our town had a major flood. The building department was backed up for many weeks—if not months—and during that time we were doing a full renovation on a house. So we called the inspector and they said, "We can't make it out there for at least two or three weeks." We couldn't stop progress on the house, however, so we took pictures of the walls before we put the Sheetrock up, took pictures of the Sheetrock, the wiring, plumbing, SKUs, and all the materials we were using. By the time they got to the job site, we were done, and they said, "Gentlemen, we have a problem here. The job is done." We said, "No problem. You guys were busy, so we tried to make your job easy. Here are pictures of everything we did." We showed them every room, every picture, and because we had a trusting relationship with them, they looked over everything we'd documented and said, "Okay, this is good. We're going to go ahead and sign off on this property now." Had we not known them or had we tried to skirt around them in the past—had we not incorporated them into our team from the get-go—they probably would've red-flagged that job and made us rip everything out to prove what had been done.

Punch-Out Crew

Sometimes contractors get 95 percent of the way done and don't come back. This is why you should never pay a contractor until they're done. When this happens, sometimes they will leave a punch-out worker around the house. This person is there to finish the many little things that might take two or three days to do, but a contractor doesn't deem worthy of their time. If they don't have someone, you should have your own punch-out crew or handyman who can come and do odds and ends on a job site.

Cleaning Team

When you're done with a job, contractors *should* clean the house, but contractors aren't good cleaners. They do an okay job, not a great job. Therefore, consider having a professional cleaning crew come in. Get all the dust out of the cracks and crevices, clean out things like your filter, furnace, or air conditioning unit. Then have them go through and clean the inside of cabinets, drawers, and all the places where there's dust. It might cost you a few hundred dollars, but that house will look and smell immaculate, and that's what you want when you're getting ready to sell or rent it.

Photographer

The recommendation used to be that you should have a professional photography crew come in and take pictures of your house. With the invention of great cameras on mobile phones, however, you can do it yourself—but you'll still need to keep lighting and other photography skills in mind—or you can hire someone to come out and take pictures for you. Pro tip: Because you're doing renovations, you're going to want to have before and after pictures. Take them from multiple angles in every room, and make sure the before and after pictures are all taken from the exact same angles. There's nothing worse than seeing a before and after picture when you can't even tell it's the same room.

Listing Agent

Once you're done with the renovation process, you'll need a listing agent to list the house. Since you'll have a real estate agent to help you buy the house, your listing agent could be the same person. Either way, you'll need a listing agent to list your house for sale, and a property management company if you're going to rent the house.

Accountant

There's nothing worse than having a box full of receipts come tax time, which is why you need a good tax accountant. For business owners, H&R Block or your local tax accountant who does W-2 tax returns isn't going to cut it. There are so many legal tax deductions you can take advantage of as a business owner—and if you flip a house or buy a rental, you *are* a business owner. Once again, referrals are the absolute best way to find a good accountant, and after you do, interview them, make sure you like them, and also ensure they understand your world as a real estate investor.

TEAM MEMBERS YOU NEED TO SCALE YOUR BUSINESS

Who do you need to help you scale your business?

Business Coach

First and foremost, you'll need a business coach—somebody who knows what you're trying to do in order to help you learn, scale, and grow. Having a coach or mentor will help you find the necessary time because they will make you a better business owner. And there are people who are willing to give you advice. And advice is one thing, but a paid coach or a paid mentor is crucial for scaling your business.

Marketing Team

Next, you want to have lead generation methods in place, since this allows you to have more coming in on a regular basis to buy more houses or get more rentals. This means you'll need to have a marketing person or team because you can only drive for dollars yourself so much. If you want to scale, you're going to have to sub that out and invest some money back into your business to create lead generation funnels via marketing sources. Enter the marketing team.

Virtual and/or Personal Assistant

You can hire a virtual assistant (VA) through websites like Upwork, Fiverr, or other online sources. Thanks to the virtual world we live in, we now have access to some very talented people all over the globe. When you find the right fit, they can be an incredible help to you in your business. And because of the amount of competition globally, their rates are very affordable.

When we had about five flips going at once in our third year, we finally hired our first personal assistant, who came to our house every day from 10 a.m. to 3 p.m. We were living in a two-bedroom condo, and she worked at our kitchen table, doing everything from turning power on in properties and making phone calls to contractors, to making sure the receipts were getting put in the right place. All those simple things that bog you down, those things if you don't do, wind up becoming monster problems. You can also get an answering service where someone answers your phones twenty-four hours a day to ensure people can always reach you.

Project Manager

We have one project manager that manages all of our construction projects. We used to do it ourselves, but as you start to scale, you may want to consider hiring a project manager, too. They'll hire all the contractors, manage all the contractors, and manage the job site from the time you say, "Here's the house I bought" to when you say, "Hey, go develop a scope of work and put this house together." A project manager is one of the most valuable team members you can have once you start experiencing multiple projects at once. A project manager will also take away all the headaches so that you can focus on the most important things: finding deals and then building and managing your team.

Property Management Company

We know we've said it before, but when you have rentals, don't be the landlord. If you have a professional property management company as your partner, they get paid to handle all those potential problems for you.

The more you subcontract work out, the more work you can get done on a regular basis—and the more rentals you can buy. Remember: When other people are doing the work for you, the more extra time you have and the faster you can build your wealth as a real estate investor. Always bear in mind that one of the secrets to wealth is to build the right team so *you're* not doing the day-to-day work; you're just focusing on the big picture. The bottom line is, there are people that are a lot better than you at a lot of things. Take advantage of that and delegate. Build and manage a strong, loyal team, and you'll also build an amazing business.

CHAPTER 13

NEXT-LEVEL INVESTING: BECOME A PRIVATE LENDER

The next level of becoming a real estate investor is to be on the funding side of the deal. In Chapter 4 we talked about how you'll have to pay higher rates because investors take a higher risk. This means you may have to pay two to five points (a point is 1 percent of the amount of the loan) upfront for borrowing the money, and then a 10 to 14 percent annual percentage rate. It might be a six-month minimum or one-year minimum; it all depends on the lender. But instead of paying 10 to 14 percent and two to five points, what if you could *earn* 10 to 14 percent and two to five points?

The other side of real estate investing is a passive investment with a very high return. Most people are happy making a 4 to 6 percent return in the stock market. If they ever do as good as making 10 percent consistently month after month, year after year, they're thrilled with it. But I'm talking about making a whole lot more than that by investing in real estate, and there are a couple ways you can do it.

To fund the deal, you can either use the cash you have, or set up a self-directed IRA and lend money out of it. How? If you have IRA or retirement funds that are qualified to be put into a self-directed IRA— do it. Use a third-party fiduciary company that will make sure you're compliant with the IRS, too. You don't want to mess around and try and do it yourself. Pay the fee to use an outside company that will ensure that your account is maintained and your money stays tax-deferred or tax-free, depending on if it's a traditional IRA or if it's a Roth IRA.

SETTING YOUR TERMS

When working with real estate investors as a private lender, it's important to find experienced investors that you trust, keeping in mind that newer investors are higher risk. I recommend you invest in an area or town that you know, preferably somewhere you've already worked or invested in. The deal you set up after you find an investor or investors you want to work with is up to you. *You* set the terms. It could be 8 percent, 10 percent, 12 percent, 15 percent, a three-month minimum, a six month-minimum, a twelve-month minimum, or no minimum. You could do a credit check or not, require additional collateral or properties they already own, do 100 percent financing, 80 percent financing, or 50 percent financing. You could do construction loans and pay them out in draws as the work is inspected. Or you could simply loan people a lump sum of money up front for the renovation and the purchase price, with the expectation of a return. In your return, you can also define the terms. You could have a monthly payment of interest only, or you could amortize it over a period of time and get monthly payments. Most private lenders do an interest-only payment and then balloon for the principal at the end of the term. Most terms are no more than a year (although sometimes they can be two years), and the money is loaned at short-term rates.

A Real-Life Example

We recently helped out a young couple doing their first flip; they were a referral from a close, lifelong friend of ours. This couple was of good moral fiber and had a lot of character, honesty, and integrity, and we got to know them over the course of a year. When it came time for them to do their flip, we loaned them the money. They needed to borrow $100,000 on this property and had about $30,000 of their own money in the deal from some home equity they had. We were the only lender on the deal, so we were in first position. This meant our mortgage was the first one to be paid in the event of a default. (So, if we had to go to foreclosure or anything catastrophic happened, we were in first position. In fact, I recommend that you always put yourself in first position, and if you have to go in second position, charge more for that and be very cautious—especially if you're working with a new investor.)

Next, we had a lawyer do a title search on the property—*always* have a lawyer do this for you. The borrower paid the attorney's fee to do the title work, prepare the note, prepare the mortgage, and file the mortgage. If they want to borrow the money, the borrower is going to pay all the fees, just like they would with a bank loan. They also pay all the closing costs to the attorney to borrow that money. It might cost them $2,000 to $3,000 for all those fees, but this will ultimately depend on your state and county. For the $100,000 loan, we charged them 2.5 points and a 12 percent annual percentage rate. The 2.5 points—or loan origination fee—was $2,500. They were hoping to be done in nine months, but had a few problems with their renovations, so they used that money for a full year, which benefited us. When they sold their house, we had already received our $2,500 up front, got the $100,000 back, and then—because we charged 12 percent interest—we got an additional $12,000 as a lump sum. At the end of the day, we made $14,500 on a $100,000 investment; that's a 14 percent annual percentage rate of return. That's good—and was also backed by a piece of real estate.

There's a short-term risk in a deal like this; however, a short period of time when you loan them more than the property's worth during the renovation cycle. But that's why they're paying a higher interest rate. If you do this, make sure they send you pictures so you can see the renovations. Every week, check in to make sure things are happening. I recommend that you stay on top of them until you build a trust level with the people you invest in. At the end of the third week, that house was worth more than

$100,000 because they'd done enough renovations. When they finally finished renovating, the house was worth more than we had invested in it, so we were secured by a piece of real estate. Additionally, they had an insurance policy which listed them as insured, but also listed our lending entity as an additional insured entity. Therefore, if anything changed in the policy or the policy was canceled, we'd be notified. If any payouts happened, we'd get paid. All in all, we had an investment backed by a hard asset—a piece of property—and by insurance.

Documents

There are a few documents you'll want to have in place that your lawyer will draw up. One is a note; this document lays out exactly what the terms are. Using the example above, the terms were that the borrower was going to pay 2.5 points upfront, borrow $100,000, pay 12 percent interest as a lump sum when the deal closed, and pay a minimum of six months interest.

The second document is the mortgage. This is the legal instrument filed at the county that ties you to the title. Therefore, if anything worse case were to happen and they pulled that mortgage, they would check to see the first person who's owed money is you. And remember, you also have the insurance documents protecting you, and your lawyer or title company has done the previous due diligence to make sure there are no other liens on the title.

BRIDGE LENDING

I recommend becoming a private lender after you've done a few deals yourself, because when *you* do it, you'll understand the process better. When you can help other people get started in this business, it's an amazing feeling, and each party can make an amazing rate of return while being fully protected. If you want to start small, first become a bridge lender. A bridge lender uses what's called a bridge loan. Let's say the person who wants to borrow money went to a hard-money lender and the lender was willing to lend them 80 percent of the deal. This means they still have to come up with $25,000 on their own. If they don't have it, you can actually be a bridge lender—which is riskier. Let's say you loan them $25,000 on the deal so they can get the mortgage—you're covering the bridge, which is why it's called bridge or gap funding.

Recently, one of our students put a deal together. He needed $25,000 and asked us if he could borrow it. We told him, "You can borrow the $25,000. But when we get it back in six months, you're going to owe us $30,000."

To which he replied, "Wow, that's an awful high expense rate of return."

"But I'm taking a risk," I said. "Keep in mind, I'm in second position. If the deal goes south, I could lose $25,000. So I need to get paid for that risk."

He agreed. We asked him to use another piece of property—one he owed outright—to collateralize that money so that we were still protected. Additionally, when we lent him the money, we put a clause in the mortgage saying that there was going to be a penalty if he went past the deadline. In this particular case, it was $1,000 a month. When he sold the deal, he gave us the $25,000 back, plus an additional $5,000, and another $1,000 because he paid us one month late. In the end, we loaned him $25,000 and got back a $6,000 return in six months—that's a 24 percent return on the money in only six months. At an annualized rate of return, that would be 48 percent. What a great way to make amazing income as a lender on a short-term investment!

If you don't have the cash available but have home equity, advances on credit cards, or a line of credit, you can invest that and get a greater rate of return than you'd pay to borrow that money. Just make sure the deal makes sense. If it's a short-term loan, you can charge whatever you want to charge, but if it's a long-term loan and you start building a pool of people who you can invest with, you can start to give *them* money to do their flips. We charge a premium for that money, but we are there to help them get started in their business. You can do this too as a lender. Lend them your cash, your self-directed IRA, or the money you get from any credit lines you have. They'll pay you a higher rate of return, which creates another awesome way for you to build wealth. If you do this right, you could start making 12 to 15 percent on average every year on your money, and keep turning it over and over and over—all while secured by a piece of real estate. You don't do the work—you're not a contractor—all you are is a private lender on the property, and that means you can make some serious coin and some serious rates of return.

DOS AND DON'TS

Do make sure you're in first position when you loan the money.

Do ensure you have insurance and that you're listed as an additional insured.

Do make sure that you have an attorney do the papers for you and oversee the entire process, including the note and mortgage.

Do ensure that it's all done on the up and up—these are not handshake deals.

Do ensure that the person borrowing pays all the fees that you might incur.

Do always make sure you know what terms you want; if you want to collect payments, not collect payments, interest-only payments, to get the principle at the end, do six months minimum, three months, etc.—*you* set the terms. If you are in second position on one of those gap or bridge funding loans, make sure you do have some other security from that person if they have it. If not, then charge them more.

Do put your money to work and pull it out every year at 10 to 16 percent. Your money will double every five years if you're earning a 14.4 percent interest rate annually.

Don't be involved in finding people to invest in yourself. Instead, find a fund that will put your money to work in real estate investing for you. They'll do the legwork and research and will use other people's money to get the return. Sometimes you can get a piece of ownership, long-term returns, or short-term returns—those are all dependent on the fund and the type of investment that they're involved in. The only drawback is you don't really have a say about what's going on in the overall grand scheme of things, because there are several investors who create the security. In other words, you won't have a direct line to the property owner to see what's going on, but it is a great way to be a truly passive income investor.

You can also do it through the stock market with a REIT, or real estate investment trust (but remember, we're trying to get you out of the stock market in the first place!), but your rates of return won't be nearly as good as if you find private equity funds to work with. Additionally, you can do it yourself by investing in people who are starting their own businesses, or who are already in the business of doing the work. A lot of professionals, even like us, are always looking for money to do more deals in our business. Our investors have earned millions of dollars in interest over the past fourteen years, and they currently earn a 10 percent rate of return on their money. We pay less than other people, because we have such a strong track record, and they feel very secure. In fact, one of our investors recently told us, "I love investing in you because I sleep well at night."

When you build that kind of reputation with people, you'll have that money and it will be very easy. Become a lender, and if you get the right relationship going, you too will be able to sleep really well at night knowing that you could have very high interest rates and double your money in five years or less.

CHAPTER 14

DON'T JUST MANAGE THROUGH A CRISIS— AMASS WEALTH

In 2020, our business was doing pretty well. We had our speaking and education business, and had just put $80,000 into infomercials, radio commercials, local news stations, and online ads for a local education event. Then COVID hit, and the governor of New York declared a state of emergency and decided that nobody could get together. We owned a seminar company with multiple employees and were making millions of dollars, and yet we couldn't hold a seminar. We realized then that we were going to be out of business, and we didn't have any idea for how long. At first, it was going to be fourteen days to flatten the curve, but now it's years later and the pandemic is still going on.

When COVID first struck, we laid around and licked our wounds for about six weeks; we had no idea what to do. We couldn't believe that our education and coaching business was being shut down and we were being forced to not have seminars or workshops anymore. What in the world were we supposed to do? But then we thought to ourselves, "We've made it through one global crisis, and now we're staring down another one." Remember, we'd started our business in the macro crisis of the real estate crash, and here we were again, ironically having just lost another $80,000.

So, we decided to double down once more.

We saw an ad for someone doing seminars online and thought to ourselves, "There is no way that's going to work. Who in their right mind is going to sit for three days on a webinar? That sounds incredibly boring." Then we called our marketing company, had some conversations, one thing led to another, and we decided to try it with the people who had already purchased their tickets for our local event. We had about thirty-eight people attend and found out that if we did it right—with the right camera angles, production crew, AV team, and music—we could recreate the experience of being in person over Zoom. What an amazing three days we had! We ended up enrolling around fourteen students from that workshop and have been able to change their lives ever since. It also changed *our* lives, too, because we found out your worst day can be your best day, and you just don't know it yet—all you have to do is double down. It's like being at a casino: You don't know you're going to win, but sometimes you double down based on what you think might happen and just trust your gut.

We doubled down with everything we had and went to work.

After that experience, we told our team, "We're going to continue doing virtual events, even when the world opens up. We want to stay virtual because we think that people want to stay home and learn. We know that *we* want to stay home and learn!" Before the pandemic, we were traveling a lot to do our Home Flipping Workshops in different parts of the country. Even though we were only gone for about five days per month, in a year those sixty days—or two months—on the road added up.

And as much as we love doing in-person events, there was nothing quite like having an education company that we could run from our office and be able to be home with our children at night. Just as importantly, our team could be home with *their* children. I didn't like when education companies drove around town and went out and told everybody, "Hey, being a real estate investor is an amazing way of living. You have so much free time. You can do so many things. You have total freedom." Yet those same people were traveling forty-eight weeks out of the year and never even saw their kids.

We thought to ourselves, "That's hypocritical, and that's not the kind of company we want to build."

In the end, our worst day became our best day because we leaned into the crisis. We transitioned into the virtual space and are now dominating it, providing education and coaching. Does it have its challenges? Absolutely. Do we have small crises all the time? Of course. Is it perfect? No way. But is it better than what most people in our space are doing? Definitely. When you have a crisis arise in your life, whatever it might be, it's really important that you take a look and say, "What am I going to do, and how can I double down on this?" Because life's going to go on anyway. You're still going to have the same goal you had before you went into the crisis when you're *in* the crisis, and when it passes, the only question is: Will you take steps towards it?

HELPING PEOPLE DURING CRISES

As real estate investors, we're dealing with people that are in crisis *all the time*. That's where the money really is for us, when we find people in crisis mode. Remember, the Ds of motivated sellers are death, disease, divorce, downsized, disgusted, disaster, dilapidated, deserted, or decaying. During those crises, you can help these people out by buying their house. Don't think of buying people's houses during a crisis mode as taking advantage of them; think of it as helping them get out of a very tough situation by allowing them to get the equity out of their home, or, if they have no equity, getting them out of their home so they don't have that burden anymore. Who knows, you might be helping yourself out of a crisis at the same time, like we did when we got started.

During a global crisis, foreclosures also tend to increase. The government has been very active in injecting free money into our economy. Unfortunately, that is going to cause a major problem when people who have not been able to pay their mortgages without that additional assistance are going to have to pay their mortgage again—on their own. That's going to create more foreclosures, which is going to be a massive opportunity because in the middle of a crisis *is* massive opportunity if you know how to play your cards right. You can buy a house from someone and help them get out of a tough situation while also making an incredible living and building wealth for yourself at the same time. Instead of putting your head in the sand and waiting for a crisis to pass you by, use it to your advantage.

A tornado recently went through Kentucky four miles away from where one of our students lives. While it was an absolutely horrible situation, we reminded our student that in any crisis there is opportunity. People are going to start getting insurance payments in the coming months for houses where the roof was torn off, the side of the house is gone, or the house is gone altogether. People are going to get their insurance money, and then they may not want to live in their house anymore. They will also probably be willing to let their property go for next to nothing. We've experienced this when we buy houses with fire damage; the sellers get a large chunk of money from their insurance company, and they let their property go for next to nothing because they've already received their payout. The sale price is just bonus money to them. Therefore, in our student's case, she could put those houses under contract and sell the land off to other investors who want to rebuild.

At the end of the day, our job as investors is to look for the next opportunity and double down on it for ourselves, then to help those experiencing their own crisis out while making a profit in the process. That way, you can not only manage through a crisis, by actually amass tremendous wealth during it.

CHAPTER 15

DON'T LET OPPORTUNITY PASS YOU BY

If we can push through, double down, and have it pay off *big* for us, you can, too. We didn't know what we were doing, we just knew we wanted a better life for our family and had to find a better way to live. We weren't prepared for retirement, but we knew we wanted to spend more time with our kids and live in our dream home in Florida on the ocean. Well, last year we actually bought that home, and now we live on the ocean. We have dolphins in our backyard, and it has become an amazing life, and it all happened because of real estate.

There's a common response when people ask when the best time to invest in real estate is: "Twenty years ago." But what's the next best time to invest in real estate? Right now. Right now is the best time, because right now will be twenty years ago in twenty years. Some of you will look back and say, "It was the best decision I ever made," and we hope this book was able to help you at least understand all the different ways you can get involved in real estate investing.

As we write this book, we are still in the COVID crisis, and it'll probably be going on for a while yet. During this time, a lot of governments have allowed millions of people to not pay their mortgages or their rent, and that's caused a crisis that's like a can being kicked down the road. There is going to come a time when those mortgages and that rent will be due, and it won't be far off. Many banks will find ways to help people restructure their loans and get back on track, but people who haven't been able to pay their mortgage for years now are going to start sinking into foreclosure.

It's the same thing that happened back in 2008 during the financial crisis: the foreclosure rate was skyrocketing because people were losing their houses, and we believe the same thing's going to happen again. It won't be at quite the same rate as 2008, but it will happen. We've been on a bull run for almost fourteen years now in the real estate market—ever since 2008—and they are cyclical. Almost every ten years they readjust. Inflation's at an all-time high right now, and your best hedge against that is real estate investing. If you can position yourself to take advantage of it, you will be in the best shape of your life five, ten, and twenty years from now.

Think about it this way: If you're a surfer and walk into the water, hold your surfboard, stand still, and a big wave comes in, what's going to happen? It's going to knock you right over. However, if you're paddling the same direction as the wave and get ready for it, then when that wave comes in, you're already in motion and able to ride that sucker all the way in—and enjoy it. That's what's going to happen to some of you. Some of you will stand still and nothing will happen; you'll stand right there, watch the real estate market turn, and watch all kinds of opportunities come, but you won't be ready, and this opportunity will run you right over.

Others will take action and get started as a real estate investor right now.

Ask yourself: What would you do with your life if you had an extra $50,000 a year from flipping one house, part time, alongside your job? What would you do if you could do two houses a year and make an extra $100,000 on top of your job? Would you leave your job? Would you keep your job? Would you pay off debt? Would you prepare for retirement? Would you get yourself in a better place for retirement? Have you ever even thought about how much you need to retire comfortably?

PLANNING FOR RETIREMENT

How much you need to retire comfortably may not be a number you want to think about, but you should. You can't just ignore the problem and hope it goes away. If you don't do anything, if you don't take advantage of where we are in the country right now with real estate investing, you will kick yourself five, ten, and even twenty years from now. So let's talk about how much you think you're going to need for retirement. Let's assume that you want to get a 5 percent rate of return when you're retired; that's a safe investment, and not too risky. To get there, how much do you have to have per month in retirement? And remember: that's what it's worth today, not twenty years from now, when inflation will have increased.

If you want to live on $5,000 a month, then you're going to have to make $7,000 a month to retire, pre-tax. That $7,000 a month times twelve months is

$84,000 a year. Next, divide the annual income you need to earn for retirement by the interest rate you're going to achieve. If you're going to get a 5 percent rate of return on a secured investment, divide 84,000 by 5 percent. That number is $1,680,000. That's how much you have to have in retirement savings in order to be able to retire with $5,000 a month—and that's in today's currency. Now think about it: Do you think $5,000 is going to cover it? Most of us are probably going to need at least $10,000 a month to survive. That means you're going to have to have well over $3 million in savings to live off the interest because people are living longer now, which is the good news. The bad news is living longer costs more money. What's the worst thing that can happen? You run out of money before you die—and that's probably why people die early.

MEET KATHY

Kathy is a cancer survivor and came to us with two apartments under her belt. On the third or fourth coaching meeting we had with her personally, we noticed that her hair was falling out and asked what happened. Kathy told us that she was suffering from breast cancer and was in chemo. She had just lost her sister to a different kind of cancer a week earlier. We asked, "Kathy, why in the world are we on a coaching call for real estate?" She looked at us and said, "Because I'm going to live." She became our hero at that moment because she showed us what it takes to be successful in life. No matter what life throws at you, you have to decide to grab an opportunity and go with it, because opportunities like this don't go away—they just go to somebody else. Kathy decided she was going to make it happen for her. She's now flipped over $500,000 worth of profits in the past two years and has built a $15,000 per month rental income portfolio with our guidance. We're so proud of what she's done.

PAM PART 2

You met Pam in Chapter 2; she tried to do two rental properties before coming to us and actually lost both of them. It was a bad situation. For fifteen years, her two daughters kept pushing her to try again in real estate investing, so she finally found us, and we helped her discover the courage to try again. She ended up making over $60,000 in total on her first wholesale and flip and left her job early. She's now done over $300,000 worth of flips and makes over

$4,000 a month in rental income. She just informed us that she's in the process of putting together a $6 million, twenty-unit build she's going to do for herself to improve her neighborhood, help her community, and build wealth for herself. We are so proud of her, too. Like us, she's an average person; she didn't come from money, but she was determined to change the legacy of her and her children's lives.

MEET JOSH AND CRYSTAL

Josh and Crystal were small business owners that had a small pool business. They came to us when they were at a point in life where they were about to sell their dream home because they couldn't afford it anymore. They loved it; they planned to fill it with babies, but they couldn't figure out how to afford the house and the taxes until they started becoming real estate investors. Now, in the past two years, they've done three flips over $150,000 in profit, and they just did a wholesale where they made $30,000 in profit. Now they talk at our events and they share their story of how they were able to stay in their dream home because of real estate investing. This all happened because they saw an opportunity and decided to take advantage of it.

MEET SUSAN

Susan was a corporate executive for a large commercial investing firm. She came to one of our workshops and decided that day to go full time. I do not recommend that, but she was sick and tired of not having time with her kids. Because she traveled so much, she missed their soccer games and baseball games, and she was frustrated. She made a decision to walk away from a six-figure salaried job to become a full-time real estate investor with no experience. We coached her and helped her through that time to shorten her learning curve, but let us tell you, she was an amazing inspiration. She's gone on to flip over $300,000 on over eight flips in the past two and a half years. Now she talks to us from the soccer games. She's on her phone and making deals, all while spending time with her family. That's what's most important to her.

MEET LISA

Lisa was a hospice nurse who cared for people in the last days of their lives. She was used to hearing all the stories about all the regrets people had about all the opportunities they squandered in their lives. At some point, we all get to the point where our bodies and/or our minds will not let us go any further. For some of us, that time comes earlier, for others later, but that's the one guarantee in life. That's why we have to decide what kind of a legacy we want to leave behind. And when do we want to start? Because at some point, we're out of time.

Lisa used to spend time with these people in their last days; some were fulfilled, but a lot were not. They hadn't reached their goals or didn't go for their dreams, and their biggest regret was that they didn't take advantage of opportunities or the things that came their way. They just wanted to play it safe. They didn't want to put in any extra effort, step outside of the norm, or be different. Because people that go off in search of their goals and dreams are different—we *are* a different kind of people.

As time went on, Lisa developed a very aggressive type of breast cancer, one that almost killed her. She saw an infomercial we ran, came to one of our workshops fresh off of being on chemo, and sat in the front row. She was determined to be a successful real estate investor. She realized there were a lot of people in that room who were average people who had to grind to get where we were. She was inspired that if we could do it, she could do it, too, and so she did. Lisa has gone on to flip four houses, making her $180,000 in profit, and has built over $1,500 worth of rental income per month. She went on to become a full-time real estate agent and always says, "Make your excuses your reasons." In other words, stop making excuses for your life, excuses for why you can't be successful, excuses for why you can't do this or don't have the time to do that. Stop making excuses and turn your excuses into reasons why *you should* do something. If you say you don't have the time and that's your excuse, you should start saying, that's my reason. I have to become a real estate investor because I don't have any time and I want to own my time. If you say I don't have any money, then that's why you should become a real estate investor, because you want to have money.

What we do is *work*—it's not easy—but it's absolutely worth it. What we can do for you is help you fold time. If you decide to come to one of our workshops or see us in person, we can help you with our coaching programs to fold time. Fold time means that when you learn from others who have gone before you, you can get to your goals much faster as they help you navigate landmines and share their experiences to speed up your own process, thereby folding time in half in many cases. We recently had one of our students who's a realtor tell us that it would have taken her a minimum of three to five years to connect all the dots, but using our coaching helped her connect the dots in one to two years, which gave her her time back. If you don't want to waste your time figuring something out, but prefer to get coached or mentored so you can get on with living your life faster, take advantage of the opportunity that's in front of you right now.

What do you want to do? What do you want to leave for your family? What kind of a legacy do you want to leave behind? Do you want to go in the ground and just be gone? Or do you want to leave behind a financial legacy and change the course of your family's life? It takes one generation to change your family's history, and I think most of us want our kids to have better lives than we have. Well, that takes time, work, energy, a system, and persistence. But we'll tell you from experience—and from those of our thousands of students—if people put the work in, they can totally change their lives, and so can you.

We want to live a great life, but we also want to leave a financial legacy for our family. Although we don't believe that money will bring happiness, we believe a lack of money can add tremendous stress to one's life. It's very difficult to be happy when you're thinking about a lack of money all the time. Money doesn't make you good or bad, it just makes you more of what you already are. If you're someone who's generous, giving, and has a prosperous mindset, when you have money, that's what you'll be. You'll give more, help more, and think about how you can help other people and how you can give back. If you're a miserable kind of a person, guess what money does to you? It usually makes you more of a jerk, or into someone who's controlling.

Therefore, as you're thinking about what kind of legacy you want to leave, ask yourself what kind of a person you are. I bet you don't want to leave your job to your family. Most people don't even *like* their job. But what if you could leave a business, a rental portfolio of 5, 10, 50, 100, 500, or 1,000 rental units that pay thousands or tens of thousands or hundreds of thousands a month in income? That's a different story. After you build rental income, it doesn't disappear. You can create passive income so when you leave this earth, that income and legacy can be passed onto your children. And if you have the right team members in place, you can make sure that you structure everything so that the taxes aren't passed on to your kids.

Real estate investing is by far the best way for average people like you and me to build an amazing life and leave an amazing legacy for our families.

Our advice is to not let this opportunity of a lifetime pass you by. Don't be the person looking back in five years and saying, "Wow, I should have done that." There were a lot of people back in 2014 and 2015 who looked back and said, "Wow, I wish I got started when you guys did back in 2008." We're telling you right now that if you do nothing, you'll look back in five years and say, "Oh my God, I really wish I got started in 2022."

Don't be the person who looks back and says, "I wish I had." Instead, be excited; be the person to say, "Boy, I'm so glad that I did that when I did!"

We hope this book sets you off in the right direction, helps you get and stay on that path, and allows you to realize that average people can have an awesome life through real estate investing.

ACKNOWLEDGMENTS

We want to thank all of those who have been on this wild ride with us, making our journey a successful one thus far. We have only just begun!

Thank you to Janey for believing in us when no one else did, and for taking a risk to be our first private investor, using your home equity line of credit. Thank you also for your continued investment over all these years. Without you, this journey may have never happened!

Thank you to Bruce and Cindy for your loyalty over the years and for trusting us with your investment. Thank you for the introduction to so many of your friends, who also became private lenders. You're the reason we were able to scale so quickly. We value your friendship and have from the first time you took up a collection when our first son was born over twenty-two years ago. You have always been there for us, and we appreciate you both very much.

Thank you to all of our loyal private investors. Without you, we couldn't move as fast as we have over the years.

Thank you to all of our incredible team at Signature Home Buyers for pivoting during COVID, moving to a virtual model, and allowing us to relocate to Florida and live our dream while you continue to grow the business we created. We appreciate all of you very much.

Thank you to Jeff for your incredible dedication in helping us get VestorPRO off the ground. For taking me to lunch that one day and pushing me to start my lifelong dream of a coaching business. For being there in the early days, when no one showed up for presentations. For sacrificing long weekends away from your family when we had virtually no success, and still laughing and working through it. For helping us set up tables and chairs, serving water to guests, and for brainstorming ideas at all hours of the day and night. Basically, for always doing whatever it takes. You have been our rock, and one person we can always count on during this journey. Words cannot describe our appreciation of you, Nicole, and your girls, who have always supported us behind the scenes on this journey. The best is yet to come, my friend.

Thank you to our dear friends Gerald and Beth, who opened our eyes to the possibilities in the coaching and education space, and how to do it right for longevity. For allowing us to bring your daughters onto to the team to support us, and most importantly, for always inspiring me to change lives, like you've been doing for years. And for reminding me always that, "We get to *do* this!"

Thank you to all of our amazing team at VestorPRO and to all of you who help us with our Home Flipping Workshops, as well as coaching and helping our students with excellence. Thank you to everyone who trusted our leadership when we went 100 percent virtual to survive the pandemic. Who knew we would be this successful after COVID almost shut us down? We're changing lives together, including our own. We appreciate and value each and every one of you.

Thank you to all of our coaches and mentors over the years who have helped us fold time and reach our goals so much faster.

Thank you to all of our children for tolerating us while we've been grinding out this dream. A special thank you to our oldest son, Dakota, who started by editing our marketing videos when he was only thirteen, and has worked in all areas of our companies ever since. He now manages our entire Short Term Rental business, and manages our Zoom room at our virtual Home Flipping Workshops. Also thank you to Peyton who recently joined us to help send out packets to all attendees! We're very proud to have our son and daughter with us on this journey and hopefully the others will join us too! Thank you Dakota, Peyton, Chasity, and Cruz, we love all of you. You are our "WHY."

And finally, thank you to all of our lifelong close friends: Becky, Pat, Ruthie, Chad, Bryan, Terry, Paul, and Erin, who knew us when we were sleeping on an air mattress in a small condo, and who have been with us on every step of the journey—both good and bad—and never treated us differently no matter how much success we've had. We love you all. You're the best!

ABOUT THE AUTHORS

Glenn and Amber Schworm have taught thousands of people their simple home flipping formula at their Home Flipping Workshop. They continue to flip houses as they help people change their lives by teaching them how to "Find, Fund, Fix, Flip, and Hold" properties to create immediate cash flow, while also teaching them how to find and set up assets that generate long-term passive income. They live in North Redington Beach, FL, with their four kids.